AF270781

Photo by Carol Rosegg/Martha Swope Associates
A scene from the Lamb's Theatre production of "Johnny Pye." Set design by Peter Harrison

JOHNNY PYE

A Musical

Based on the Short Story
"Johnny Pye and the Foolkiller"
STEPHEN VINCENT BENÉT

Book and Lyrics by
MARK ST. GERMAIN

Music and Lyrics by
RANDY COURTS

★

★

DRAMATISTS
PLAY SERVICE
INC.

Copyright, © 1994, by Mark St. Germain and Randy Courts

CAUTION: Professionals and amateurs are hereby warned that JOHNNY PYE is subject to a royalty. It is fully protected under the copyright laws of the United States of America, and of all countries covered by the International Copyright Union (including the Dominion of Canada and the rest of the British Commonwealth), and of all countries covered by the Pan-American Copyright Convention and the Universal Copyright Convention, and of all countries with which the United States has reciprocal copyright relations. All rights, including professional, amateur, motion picture, recitation, lecturing, public reading, radio broadcasting, television, video or sound taping, all other forms of mechanical or electronic reproduction, such as information storage and retrieval systems and photocopying, and the rights of translation into foreign languages, are strictly reserved. Particular emphasis is laid upon the question of readings, permission for which must be secured from the author's agent in writing.

The stage performance rights in JOHNNY PYE (other than first class rights) are controlled exclusively by the DRAMATISTS PLAY SERVICE, INC., 440 Park Avenue South, New York, N.Y. 10016. No professional or non-professional performance of the play (excluding first class professional performance) may be given without obtaining in advance the written permission of the DRAMATISTS PLAY SERVICE, INC., and paying the requisite fee.

Inquiries concerning all other rights, including original music rights, should be addressed to Mitch Douglas, c/o International Creative Management, Inc., 40 West 57th Street, New York, NY 10019.

Music written by Randy Courts for JOHNNY PYE is required for production. Please contact Dramatists Play Service for availability and fees.

SPECIAL NOTE

All groups receiving permission to produce JOHNNY PYE are required to give credit as follows:

JOHNNY PYE

Book and Lyrics by Mark St. Germain
Music and Lyrics by Randy Courts
Based on the Short Story "JOHNNY PYE AND THE FOOLKILLER"
by Stephen Vincent Benét
Originally directed by Paul Lazarus

All groups receiving permission to produce JOHNNY PYE are required to give the following acknowledgment on the title page in all programs distributed in connection with performances of the play:

"Originally produced by the George Street Playhouse,
New Brunswick, New Jersey,
Gregory S. Hurst, Producing Artistic Director,
after development as a work in progress
by the Lamb's Theatre Company,
Carolyn Rossi Copeland, Producing Director,
and the New Harmony Conference."

JOHNNY PYE AND THE FOOLKILLER was first developed as a work in progress by the Lamb's Theatre Company (Carolyn Rossi Copeland, Producing Director), and the New Harmony Conference.

JOHNNY PYE AND THE FOOLKILLER was originally produced by the George Street Playhouse (Gregory S. Hurst, Producing Artistic Director), in New Brunswick, New Jersey, in February, 1990. It was directed by Paul Lazarus; music and lyrics were by Randy Courts; book and lyrics were by Mark St. Germain; the musical director was Steven M. Alper; the set design was by William Barclay; the costume design was by Mary L. Hayes; the lighting design was by Donald Holder; the sound design was by Jim Landis and the stage manager was Thomas L. Clewell. The cast was as follows:

JOHNNY PYE	John Hickok
THE FOOLKILLER	John Jellison
YOUNG SUZY	Catherine Satterwhite
WILBUR WILBERFORCE	Tom Robbins
MRS. MILLER	Lou Williford
BARBER	Ron Lee Savin
BILL	Gordon Stanley
BOB	Larry Cahn
YOUNG JOHNNY	John Babcock
SUZY MARSH	Victoria Clark

JOHNNY PYE AND THE FOOLKILLER was produced by the Lamb's Theatre Company (Carolyn Rossi Copeland, Producing Artistic Director), in New York City, in October, 1993. It was directed by Scott Harris; music and lyrics were by Randy Courts; book and lyrics were by Mark St. Germain; musical staging was by Janet Watson; the musical director was Steven M. Alper; the orchestrations were by Douglas Besterman; the scene design was by Peter Harrison; the costume design was by Claudia Stephens; the lighting design was by Kenneth Posner; the sound design was by David Lawson and the production stage manager was David Waggett. The cast was as follows:

JOHNNY PYE	Daniel Jenkins
THE FOOLKILLER	Spiro Malas
SUZY MARSH	Katilin Hopkins
WILBUR WILBERFORCE	Peter Gerety
MRS. MILLER	Tanny McDonald
BARBER	Ralston Hill
BILL	Michael Ingram
BOB	Mark Lotito
YOUNG JOHNNY	Conor Gillespie
YOUNG SUZY	Heather Lee Soroka

CAST

YOUNG JOHNNY PYE (And Others)
YOUNG SUZY MARSH (And Others)
JOHNNY PYE (And Johnny Pye, Sr.)
SUZY MARSH (And Mrs. Marsh)
THE FOOLKILLER
BARBER (And Others)
BILL (And Others)
BOB   (And Others)
MRS. MILLER (And Others)
WILBUR WILBERFORCE (And Others)

SETTING

Martinsville, U.S.A., and various locations, 1928-1995.

CASTING NOTE

JOHNNY PYE may be performed by a cast of 10 by doubling, or by a cast of as many as 27 if each role is performed by a different actor.

If that is the case, it is still recommended that the actor who plays Young Johnny Pye also plays John Jr., and that Johnny Pye plays Johnny Pye Sr., as well.

Throughout the script, doubling suggestions are noted.

THE SET

For JOHNNY PYE's premiere performance at the George Street Playhouse, director Paul Lazarus and designer Bill Barclay created a barn like set, its many doors and loft-levels effectively framing the musical's action.

With JOHNNY PYE's New York premiere at the Lamb's Theatre, director Scott Harris and designer Peter Harrison created a landscape of rolling hills and roadways fashioned from wood planking. Perched on the hills in the distance were a series of small, folk-art-inspired sculptures such as farmhouses and windmills, which were replaced by factories and suburbs as years passed. "Time" is almost another character in JOHNNY PYE. It can be shown passing in an endless variety of ways, through subtle changes in character, costume and set pieces.

Since JOHNNY PYE moves continually through many locations from barns to battlefields, it is also possible to perform the musical on a bare stage that evokes the setting with the help of props, stools and platforms.

A simple wood plank back wall, for instance, from which necessary set pieces and chairs are hung on pegs could also be used as a backdrop.

JOHNNY PYE

ACT ONE

At rise, it is dawn. In the darkness, we see sparks. As a rooster crows, we hear the morning sounds of rural America. Lights up slowly on the Foolkiller, seated behind a grindstone, sharpening a knife. It is 1928.

SONG: ANOTHER DAY (Foolkiller, Townspeople)

FOOLKILLER. *(Sings.)*
> ANOTHER DAY
> ANOTHER DAWN
> ANOTHER MORNING
> ANOTHER GET UP GET ALONG
> AND ON YOUR WAY
> ANOTHER TASK
> ANOTHER CHORE
> YOU'VE DONE SO MANY TIMES BEFORE
> IT'S ALL TOO EASY TO IGNORE
> ANOTHER DAWN
> ANOTHER MORNING
> ANOTHER DAY

(Young Johnny Pye runs in, followed by his father, Johnny Pye, Sr. [played by Johnny Pye]. They play together. As Foolkiller sings, Barber, Bill, Bob and Mrs. Miller enter, greet each other and the day.)

FOOLKILLER.   *(Sings.)*
> ANOTHER BOY
> ANOTHER MAN
> ANOTHER FAMILY
> ANOTHER TINY TOWN TO GROW
> THE SAME AS YOU
> ANOTHER FARM
> A FIELD OF WHEAT
> A STRING OF SHOPS ALONG THE STREET
> AND ALL YOUR NEIGHBORS TURN TO GREET

        ANOTHER DAWN
        ANOTHER MORNING
        ANOTHER DAY
(Lights up on the Barber, Bill, Bob and Mrs. Miller. As they sing, Mr. Wilberforce [played by Wilbur] enters and crosses to the barbershop.)
BARBER, BILL, BOB and MRS. MILLER.   *(Sing.)*
        MARTINSVILLE GROWS TREES AND CHILDREN
        HEALTHY STRONG AND TALL
        GOT NO WORMS AT ALL
        AIR TO BREATHE AND STARS TO WISH BY
        DOGS TO SCRATCH AND FISH TO FISH BY
        GOTTA AGREE
        IT'S NOT HALF BAD TO BE
BARBER and BOB.   *(Sing.)*
        HERE IN MARTINSVILLE
BILL and MRS. MILLER.   *(Sing.)*
        HERE IN MARTINSVILLE
FOOLKILLER.   *(Sings.)*
        HERE IN MARTINSVILLE.
(Lights pull down to John Sr. and Young Johnny playing. As Foolkiller starts to grind knife, sparks fly and John Sr. is stricken, falling to the ground; crossfade to barbershop, where Mr. Wilberforce is getting his haircut.)
MR. WILBERFORCE.   I'm going up to Cruster on business and I want to look smart and sassy.
BARBER.   How long have you got? *(Young Johnny runs in, out of breath.)*
YOUNG JOHNNY.   It's Pa!
BILL.   Hold on, now!
BARBER.   Johnny!
BOB.   What's wrong, boy?
YOUNG JOHNNY.   It's my Pa. He said to send for a doctor.
BARBER.   Johnny, you stay here. *(Barber, Bill and Bob glance at each other. They cross to John Sr. joined by Mrs. Miller.)*
YOUNG JOHNNY.   *(Calling after them.)* But he says not to worry! He'll be all right! *(As Foolkiller sings, the town gathers at John Sr.'s bedside.)*
FOOLKILLER.   *(Sings.)*
        ANOTHER TIME
        ANOTHER PLACE
        ANOTHER MORNING
        WHEN SOMETHING NEW AND

VERY OLD
IS IN THE AIR
SOME TRY TO WORK
SOME TRY TO PLAY
NO MATTER WHAT THEY DO OR SAY
NO ONE CAN MAKE IT GO AWAY
ANOTHER DAWN
ANOTHER MORNING
ANOTHER DAY

MR. WILBERFORCE.   (*Readying to leave.*) Well, Johnny Pye! Your Pa better not be too sick to make his house payments.

YOUNG JOHNNY.   (*Peering at him.*) No, Sir.

MR. WILBERFORCE.   What are you looking for?

YOUNG JOHNNY.   The pole, Sir.

MR. WILBERFORCE.   "Pole?" What "Pole?"

YOUNG JOHNNY.   The pole my Pa says makes you walk funny.

MR. WILBERFORCE.   (*Advancing on him.*) You're a fool, same as he is! (*Mrs. Marsh [played by Suzy] entering with Young Suzy, intercedes.*)

MRS. MARSH.   Mr. Wilberforce, leave the boy be! (*To Suzy.*) Come along, Pumpkin. (*Mrs. Marsh and Mr. Wilberforce exit.*)

YOUNG SUZY.   Psst. Johnny? You notice anything different?

YOUNG JOHNNY.   You smell awfully clean or something.

YOUNG SUZY.   It's a new dress. I got invited to dinner. At Wilber Wilberforce's.

YOUNG JOHNNY.   You like Wilbur much? Or are you just hungry?

YOUNG SUZY.   I like him some. But he likes me. A lot. He tells me, too. All the time.

YOUNG JOHNNY.   Well, Suzy — (*Crossfade to John Sr.'s bedside. Barber, Bill, Bob and Mrs. Miller are all grouped around Young Johnny's father, blocked from view. We hear his cry.*)

JOHN SR.   Johnny!

YOUNG JOHNNY.   That's Pa! (*Mrs. Miller turns to Barber, Bill, Bob as Young Johnny runs toward them.*)

MRS. MILLER.   Don't let the boy see him like this! (*Bob holds Young Johnny, fighting to get near his father. Mrs. Marsh joins Young Suzy watching from a distance.*)

FOOLKILLER.   (*Sings.*)

SUDDENLY A WORLD SPINS
SUDDENLY A HEART STOPS
SUDDENLY A MOMENT LASTS FOREVER

AND FOREVER FALLS BEHIND
YOU REACH AHEAD
BUT FIND
YOU'RE REACHING BACK INSTEAD
WITHIN
ANOTHER SPIN
IT'S NOTHING WRONG OR RIGHT
BUT JUST ANOTHER TURNING
LIKE A DAY THAT TURNS TO NIGHT

(John Sr. reaches up his hand toward the sky.)

JOHN SR.   JOHNNY! *(Foolkiller stops wheel. Johnny leaps toward his father, reaching for him, but is stopped by Bob.)*

YOUNG JOHNNY.   PA! *(John Sr. is dead. As the town turns away, Foolkiller slowly crosses to John Sr.'s body.)*

FOOLKILLER.   *(Sings.)*

ANOTHER DAWN
ANOTHER MORNING
ANOTHER DAY

(As the town sings, Foolkiller extends his hand to John Sr., who rises and slowly exits. When tempo picks up the Foolkiller packs up, as the Townspeople resume their normal routine. Young Suzy shows Young Johnny her sympathy by giving him the ball she was playing with.)

TOWNSPEOPLE.   *(Sing.)*

MARTINSVILLE LIES IN THE HEARTLAND
SOLID AS A STONE
TAKE CARE OF OUR OWN
BUT WHAT CAN ANY BOY EXPECT
BUT CASSEROLES AND LAST RESPECTS
TINY OR GROWN ANY ORPHAN IS ALONE
HERE IN MARTINSVILLE
HERE IN MARTINSVILLE

FOOLKILLER.   *(Sings.)*

ANOTHER DAY
ANOTHER DAWN
ANOTHER MORNING
ANOTHER GET UP
GET ALONG
AND ON YOUR WAY
ANOTHER TASK

ANOTHER CHORE
YOU'VE DONE SO MANY TIMES BEFORE
IT'S ALL TOO EASY TO IGNORE
AS THEY ALL DO
IGNORING YOU

(Young Johnny suddenly turns to the Foolkiller, throwing his ball to him.)

YOUNG JOHNNY. Catch!

FOOLKILLER. *(Surprised.)* I can't do that. *(Foolkiller tosses the ball back.)*

YOUNG JOHNNY. You just did.

FOOLKILLER. *(Pause.)* You can see me?

YOUNG JOHNNY. Of course I can. You're standing right in front of me, aren't you? *(Mrs. Miller crosses to Young Johnny.)*

MRS. MILLER. Johnny Pye! What are you doing out here talking to yourself? You get on in the house, you hear? *(Mrs. Miller exits. As Young Johnny follows Mrs. Miller out, he waves to the Foolkiller.)*

FOOLKILLER. *(Waving back, sings.)*

UNTIL THIS TIME
UNTIL THIS DAY
UNTIL THIS ONE PECULIAR DAY
UNTIL THIS MORNING
UNTIL THIS DAY

(The Foolkiller disappears. Young Johnny enters tossing ball. Mrs. Miller runs in after him.)

MRS. MILLER. Johnny Pye! What are you thinking of? Give me that ball! *(She takes the ball.)* Out here playing games with your Pa just dead and buried —

YOUNG JOHNNY. He isn't dead and nobody buried him!

MR. WILBERFORCE. *(Entering.)* No back talk, boy. *(To others.)* You got to watch this one. He's a walking bad habit! Not like my boy Wilbur!

BARBER, BILL and BOB. *(As Mr. Wilberforce exits.)* The little weasel.

MRS. MILLER. *(Taking Young Johnny's cap.)* Stand up straight and push the hair out of your eyes. The way I see it, a boy's like a bushel of wheat. You gotta cut him down and grind him up before he's much use to anybody. Got that?

YOUNG JOHNNY. *(Confused.)* No, Ma'am, Mrs. Miller.

MRS. MILLER. *(Hitting him with the cap.)* Then pay attention. Or the Foolkiller will be coming to get you same as he did your Pa —

YOUNG JOHNNY. *(Taking cap back.)* My Pa's no fool! Don't you talk about my Pa that way!

BARBER. She didn't mean it, Johnny!

MRS. MILLER. Now you stay out of this, I will handle the boy!

YOUNG JOHNNY. And he didn't die! He promised he wouldn't! The Foolkiller never got my Pa! And he'll never get me! Ever! *(Young Johnny runs off.)*

BARBER.   Johnny!

MRS. MILLER.   You get back here, boy! Johnny Pye, the Foolkiller will get you now for sure. Get back here now. Right *NOW! (Pause. Barber, Bill, Bob look at Mrs. Miller.)*

BOB.   You sure did handle him. *(Lights down on them; lights up on Johnny, with bundle of clothes tied to a stick, running away. Young Suzy enters, her call stops him.)*

YOUNG SUZY.   Johnny Pye!

YOUNG JOHNNY.   Suzy, I'm running away!

YOUNG SUZY.   Where?

YOUNG JOHNNY.   *(Stops.)* Wherever you run when you're running away. *Away.*

YOUNG SUZY.   You get back here and say goodbye like a gentleman. Haven't I sat next to you all the way since kindergarten?

YOUNG JOHNNY.   Sorry, Suzy. I'm just a little jittery about getting killed and all.

YOUNG SUZY.   Who'd want to kill you?

YOUNG JOHNNY.   Mrs. Miller says the Foolkiller's going to get me, which he isn't, like he got my Pa, which he didn't. Everybody in this town thinks I'm some kind of fool not worth a spit in the lake, but they're wrong. You'll see.

YOUNG SUZY.   I don't think you're a fool, Johnny Pye.

YOUNG JOHNNY.   Thank you, Suzy. I appreciate that. I don't think you're exactly dumber than a can of dirt yourself.

SONG: GOODBYE TO JOHNNY (Young Suzy and Young Johnny)

YOUNG SUZY.   *(Sings.)*
    WILL YOU WRITE ME
YOUNG JOHNNY.   *(Sings.)*
    I WILL IF I CAN
YOUNG SUZY.   *(Sings.)*
    'CAUSE I HAVE A COLLECTION OF STAMPS IN A BOOK
    FROM ALL OVER THE WORLD AND I'D SURE LIKE TO LOOK
    AND SEE ONE OF YOUR STAMPS
    ON A PAGE IN MY ROOM
    THAT'S FROM SO FAR AWAY
    SO BE CAREFUL OKAY
YOUNG JOHNNY.   *(Sings.)*
    WILL YOU THINK OF ME

YOUNG SUZY.   (Sings.)
        YOU BET THAT I WILL
        OH I'LL THINK OF YOU JOHN EVERY ONCE IN AWHILE
        I'LL REMEMBER YOUR EYES AND REMEMBER YOUR SMILE
        AND I'LL THINK OF YOU WHEN
        YOUR CHAIR'S EMPTY AT SCHOOL
        EVERY DAY I'LL RECALL
        'CAUSE WE'RE FRIENDS AFTER ALL
        GOODBYE JOHNNY
        JOHNNY GOODBYE
        I'LL BE YOUR FRIEND
        FROM HERE TO THE END
        OF THE MOON IN THE SKY
YOUNG JOHNNY.   Guess you won't miss me much, though. With Wilbur Wilberforce around and all.
YOUNG SUZY.   I'll miss you, Johnny Pye.
YOUNG JOHNNY.   You will?
YOUNG SUZY.   More than Wilbur will.
YOUNG JOHNNY.   Oh.
BOTH.   (Sing.)
        SOMETHING'S WRONG HERE
        I FEEL AWFUL, SORT OF NERVOUS NUMB AND NAUSEOUS
        BUT ALL OVER
        AM I GONNA BE SICK
        THINK MY TONGUE'S GETTING THICK
        IT SAYS I MISS YOU
        EVEN THOUGH WE'RE HERE TOGETHER HOLDING HANDS
YOUNG SUZY.   (Sings.)
        BUT I WAS WONDERING
        WILL YOU EVER COME BACK
YOUNG JOHNNY.   (Sings.)
        YES OF COURSE I'LL COME BACK
YOUNG SUZY.   You will?
YOUNG JOHNNY.   You see this ol' tree? (Johnny begins to carve on imaginary tree.) "J.P. and ..."
YOUNG SUZY.   (Reading, excited.) That's me! (He stops.) Could you put a heart around it?
YOUNG JOHNNY.   There. I've gotta come back now. The tree says so.

YOUNG SUZY.   (Sings.)

    WILL YOU KISS ME

YOUNG JOHNNY.   (Sings.)

    I'D SURE LIKE TO TRY

YOUNG SUZY.   (Sings.)

    MAKE IT QUICK JOHNNY PYE TRY THE CHEEK ON YOUR
    RIGHT
    I WOULD GIVE YOU A LOCK OF MY HAIR LIKE A KNIGHT
    GETS FROM LADIES OF COURT WHO ARE WISHING THEM
    WELL
    BUT MY MOTHER WOULD YELL
    JOHNNY PYE

YOUNG JOHNNY.   (Sings.)

    SUZY MARSH

YOUNG SUZY.   (Sings.)

    JOHNNY PYE

MRS. MARSH.   (Off-stage.) Suzy Marsh! Get in here and make your bed! (Young Johnny runs off stage; Suzy watches him go.)

YOUNG SUZY.   (Sings.)

    GOODBYE JOHNNY
    JOHNNY GOODBYE
    I'LL BE YOUR FRIEND
    FROM HERE TO THE END
    OF THE MOON IN THE SKY
    I'LL BE YOUR FRIEND
    FROM HERE TO THE END
    OF THE LOVE IN YOUR EYE

    SOME BY THEIR DREAMS ARE ALWAYS LED
    AND SOME OF US STAY AT HOME
    TO MAKE THE BED

MRS. MARSH.   (Off stage.) Suzy! (Young Suzy runs and exits, lights down. Lights up on Foolkiller, setting up his wheel C.)

SONG: SHOWER OF SPARKS (Foolkiller)

FOOLKILLER   (Sings.)

    WATCH THE BLADE
    SCRAPE THE STONE

WATCH THE SPARKS FLY
TINY SHOWERS OF LIGHT
CUTTING THE SKY
NO TWO SPARKS ARE ALIKE
EVERY PATTERN UNKNOWN
FROM THE GRAIN OF THE STONE
FROM THE FORCE OF THE TOUCH
FROM THE SPEED OF THE WHEEL
FROM A SHOWER OF SPARKS
SEE THE WHEEL START TO TURN
WATCH THE SPARKS FLY
AND THE ACCIDENTS HAPPEN
YOU NEVER KNOW WHY
KINDLE A FIRE
PUT OUT AN EYE
EVERY ANSWER UNKNOWN
FROM THE GRAIN OF THE STONE
FROM THE FORCE OF THE TOUCH
FROM THE SPEED OF THE WHEEL
FROM A SHOWER OF SPARKS
FROM A SHOWER OF SPARKS

(Mr. Wilberforce enters R., crosses past the Foolkiller. Mr. Wilberforce is winded.)

FOOKILLER.   Hello.

MR. WILBERFORCE.   *(Sees the Foolkiller.)* How far ahead's the Cruster Inn, Mister?

FOOLKILLER.   Just a few steps 'round the bend.

MR. WILBERFORCE.   *(Stopping.)* Hot enough for you?

FOOLKILLER.   Seen it cooler. Seen it hotter, too.

MR. WILBERFORCE.   Got a Little Sammy Penknife that needs a grindstone. How much?

FOOLKILLER.   Pay what you like.

MR. WILBERFORCE.   *(Delighted.)* You drive a hard bargain. It's a deal and I'll hold you to it. Now I'm going to get me a mug of cider. *(Stops, suspicious.)* Don't you get any ideas about sneaking off, Mister. I'm quick. Real quick. *(Mr. Wilberforce exits.)*

FOOLKILLER.   Don't you worry, Mr. Wilberforce. I'll be here. *(Begins to sharpen blade. Sings.)*

SEE THE WHEEL START TO TURN
WATCH THE SPARKS FLY

(Young Johnny enters, stops when he sees Foolkiller.)

YOUNG JOHNNY.   I know you!

FOOLKILLER.   *(Evasive.)* Do you?

YOUNG JOHNNY.   Saw you back in Martinsville. You were in our yard with your grindstone. *(Puts out hand.)* I'm Johnny Pye.

FOOLKILLER.   Pleased to meet you, John.

YOUNG JOHNNY.   You too, sir. I didn't catch your name —

FOOLKILLER.   Got lots of them. I travel quite a bit, get called all kinds of names.

YOUNG JOHNNY.   *(Points to grindstone.)* You carry that with you?

FOOLKILLER.   Not always. I'm sort of a Jack of All Trades.

YOUNG JOHNNY.   That's what I need to find, Jack. A good trade. Something serious, or at least not foolish.

FOOLKILLER.   Hard to find.

YOUNG JOHNNY.   I know it. But it's the only way I'll beat the Foolkiller.

FOOLKILLER.   *(Laughs.)* The Foolkiller, is it?

YOUNG JOHNNY.   You don't believe in him?

FOOLKILLER.   You're a long way from home, Johnny Pye. Maybe you should head on back.

YOUNG JOHNNY.   No way I'm doing that. They say I'm a fool there. Said my Pa is, too. But he isn't.

FOOLKILLER.   Every man's a fool, John. Your Pa, too, no more or less than anybody else. *(Young Johnny looks at him.)*

YOUNG JOHNNY.   Do you know my Pa?

FOOLKILLER.   *(Reluctant.)* Met him once.

YOUNG JOHNNY.   You did?

FOOLKILLER.   Met your Ma, too. Long time ago.

YOUNG JOHNNY.   My Ma? Pa says I'm too young to remember her, but I do. I really do. I could tell you this one dress she wore, I can see it, like it's right here. I can remember her hugging me, even. My Pa says there wasn't anybody nicer or prettier than my Ma. Pa says all she had to do was walk into a room, and it made your day better.

FOOLKILLER.   *(Pause.)* Good people. Both of them.

YOUNG JOHNNY.   They are?

FOOLKILLER.   They were.

YOUNG JOHNNY.   You know something? About my Pa? He died. *(Young Johnny begins to cry; Foolkiller is uncomfortable.)*

FOOLKILLER.   Crying won't do much but rust metal, you know.

YOUNG JOHNNY.   I miss him so much.

FOOLKILLER.   *(Pause.)* You know, there's things that happen ... things you have to get used to, same as you do breathing or blinking, things that just happen and you can't do anything but live with them. I know you miss your Pa, John. But you had him once. That's a lot more than some folks ever get. *(Sound of Mr. Wilberforce calling.)*

MR. WILBERFORCE.　*(Off-stage.)* Hallo up there —

FOOLKILLER.　*(To Johnny.)* You have to go.

YOUNG JOHNNY.　Why?

FOOLKILLER.　Someone is coming —

YOUNG JOHNNY.　I don't mind.

FOOLKILLER.　I think it's him!

YOUNG JOHNNY.　Who?

FOOLKILLER.　The Foolkiller.

YOUNG JOHNNY.　Come with me!

FOOLKILLER.　Run, John! Run for your life and don't look back! *(Young Johnny runs off, past his bundle of clothes on a stick that he dropped coming on; he turns back. Mr. Wilberforce enters.)*

MR. WILBERFORCE.　*(To Foolkiller.)* You done yet?

FOOLKILLER.　*(Spinning wheel.)* Almost.

YOUNG JOHNNY.　*(To himself.)* Mr. Wilberforce!

MR. WILBERFORCE.　Don't expect a tip, Mister, you're cutting into my clock now. I'm a busy man, you know, I don't have all day. *(Mr. Wilberforce freezes, watching Foolkiller.)*

FOOLKILLER. *(Sings.)*

> I DON'T CARE
> WHO YOU ARE, WHAT YOU OWN
> I DON'T CARE
> IF YOU'RE YOUNG OR YOU'RE GROWN
> FOR YOU CANNOT ESCAPE WHAT IS BRED
> IN THE BONE
> I'M JUST DOING MY JOB AND
> COLLECTING THE LOAN

(Young Johnny watches with growing horror, realizing now who the Foolkiller is. The Foolkiller stops his wheel and Mr. Wilberforce falls to the ground.)

YOUNG JOHNNY.　No!

FOOLKILLER.　I told you to go. *(Young Johnny rises, looking first at Mr. Wilberforce, dead on the ground, then at the Foolkiller packing his wheel.)*

YOUNG JOHNNY.　You killed him. You're him — You're the Foolkiller!

FOOLKILLER.　Now John —

YOUNG JOHNNY.　Keep away from me!

FOOLKILLER.   John, you listen —

YOUNG JOHNNY.   You killed my father!

FOOLKILLER.   Everybody dies; there's no escaping that.

YOUNG JOHNNY.   Not me! You'll never get me! I hate you! *(Young Johnny runs off.)*

FOOLKILLER.   No escaping that, either. *(Lights down on Foolkiller and Mr. Wilberforce, lights up on barbershop; Barber, Bill and Bob. The trio watches an "off-stage" Flora Dell Drumminy. Sound of bicycle bell.)*

BARBER.   Here she comes again on that fool bicycle.

BILL.   Yep.

BOB.   Uh — huh.

BARBER.   Hey Flora Dell —

BILL.   Flora Dell —

BOB.   Flora Dell.

BILL.   *(Pause.)* Fine looking woman, that Flora Dell.

BARBER.   Sure is.

BOB.   Real fine.

BILL.   Can't hardly tell her one leg's shorter than the other.

BARBER.   No Sir.

BOB.   No way.

BILL.   Course, pine wood shrinks some when there's a dry spell. *(All stare up at sky, then down to Flora Dell's leg.)*

BOB.   Think that's why she pedals in a circle? *(Blackout on the trio, lights up on Young Johnny and Young Suzy, reading and writing letters.)*

YOUNG JOHNNY.   *(Sings.)*

    DEAR SUZY

YOUNG SUZY.   *(Sings.)*

    HE WROTE DEAR

YOUNG JOHNNY.   *(Sings.)*

    ITS PRETTY QUIET HERE

    KEEP MOVING EVERYDAY

    SO FAR I'M IN THE CLEAR

    KEEP AN EYE OUT FOR HIM COMING

    WHILE I FIGURE WHAT TO DO

    AND I HOPE THAT WEASEL WILBUR IS AS FAR AWAY FROM

    YOU

WILBUR.   *(Off stage.)* Suzy, want to come out and play? It's Wilbur!

YOUNG SUZY.   Not now, Wilbur. *(Lights out on Young Suzy, up on Young Johnny.)*

YOUNG JOHNNY.   *(Sings.)*

 HE SAYS ALL MEN ARE FOOLS

 SAYS EVERYBODY DIES

 I GUESS FROM HIM

 THAT SOUNDING GRIM

 SHOULDN'T BE A BIG SURPRISE

 BUT SINCE I'VE SEEN HIS FACE

 I'M FEELING MORE THAN FEAR

 SOMEHOW I KNOW

 WHEN IT'S TIME TO GO

 I CAN FEEL HIM WHEN HE'S NEAR....

FOOLKILLER.   *(Voice only.)* Run for your life, John, and don't look back!

YOUNG JOHNNY.   *(Sings.)*

 HOW DOES ANYONE LIVE EACH DAY

 MAKE BELIEVE WE'RE HERE TO STAY

 AND PRETEND THAT HE'S NOT ON THE WAY

 I CAN FEEL HIM IN THE AIR

 ALWAYS KNOWING, NEVER SLOWING

 DOESN'T ANYBODY SEE HE'S THERE

(Johnny hears voices.)

MRS. MILLER.   The boy's a fool, same as his father —

FOOLKILLER.   Every man's a fool, John —

YOUNG SUZY.   There's no such thing as a Foolkiller —

MRS. MILLER.   Foolkiller will get you same as he did your Pa!

YOUNG JOHNNY.   *(Sings.)*

 EVERY DAY HE GETS NEARER

 EVERY DAY I SEE CLEARER

 AS I LEARN FROM THE WORLD EVERY SAD LITTLE RULE

 EVERY DAY HE GETS BOLDER, EVERYDAY I GROW OLDER

 EVERY DAY IN THE MIRROR I STARE AT A FOOL

 AND I LEARN ALL I CAN

 AS I TURN AS I TURN AS I TURN AS I TURN

 AS I TURN AS I TURN AS I TURN

 TO A MAN

(Young Johnny and Young Suzy are replaced by their older counterparts, John and Suzy. It is now 1937.)

SUZY.   *(Sings.)*

 DEAR JOHN,

 GUESS WHAT, NOW I'M

CLERK AT THE FIVE AND DIME
WILBUR SENDS YOU HIS REGARDS
HE'S SHOPPING ALL THE TIME

(Lights up on doctor [played by Bob], and Reuben, his patient [played by Barber] stretched out on a table.)

DOCTOR.   Doctor Pye! Pressure on the femoral artery, you want him to bleed to death?

REUBEN.   *(Sitting up.)* Bleed to death?

DOCTOR.   Lay down, Reuben. You want me to sew your leg up or not? Where's that needle?

JOHN.   Here, Doctor —

REUBEN.   *(Sitting up.)* Needle?

DOCTOR.   Lay down, Reuben.

JOHN.   That was tremendous work you did, Doctor.

DOCTOR.   Well, I think we're out of the woods now. Pye, why don't you stitch him up? Reuben, you're a lucky man; you'll live to see a hundred.

JOHN.   *(Sings.)*

A DOCTOR
I WANT TO BE A DOCTOR
A MEDICAL CAREER
I KNOW I'M CUT OUT
TO CUT UP
TO STITCH AND SEVER
ASSURING
AND CURING
I'LL LIVE FOREVER
DOCTOR PYE
DOCTOR PYE
IN THESE HANDS
PEOPLE LIVE
IN THESE HANDS
THEY WILL NEVER DIE
NOT BY THE SKILLFUL HANDS
OF DOCTOR PYE

DOCTOR.   Good as new. Get up, Reuben. *(Pause. Reuben does not get up.)* Reuben?

JOHN.   Is he...?

DOCTOR.   Stone cold. *(Pause.)* Leg looks fine, though. *(Doctor covers the body; John turns away. Foolkiller enters to help the Doctor wheel the body out. John turns back, but not in time to see him. Lights up on Suzy.)*

WILBUR.   *(Off-stage.)* Suzy, want to come out and play? It's Wilbur!

SUZY.   *(Opening letter.)* Not now, Wilbur — *(Sings.)*

> DEAR SUZY
> DROP A LINE
> EXCUSE THE TURPENTINE
> I'LL BE IMMORTAL BY
> THE TIME I'M TWENTY NINE

(Lights up on Artist [played by Mrs. Miller] before easel: hands brush to John.]

ARTIST.   Bolder, Pye! You must keep your brush ahead of your brain. Let me look. *(John stands aside.)* How desolate, disturbing, dismal. I like it. You have talent, Johnny Pye. You might even have enough.

JOHN.   *(Sings.)*

> AN ARTIST
> I WANT TO BE AN ARTIST
> I THOUGHT IT WAS A DOCTOR
> BUT I WAS JUST A BOY
> REAL LIFE INDUCES
> THE JUICES
> FOR BRUSH AND CASTING
> ELATION
> CREATION
> IT'S EVERLASTING
> MASTER PYE
> MASTER PYE
> IN THESE HANDS
> MOMENTS LIVE
> IN THESE HANDS
> THEY WILL NEVER DIE
> THEY WILL NEVER DIE
> NOT IN THE GIFTED HANDS
> OF MASTER PYE

(John concludes, painting as he does so.)

ARTIST.   First rate. More than first rate, it's almost in my class. In time, this painting could become a minor classic.

JOHN.   In time, Madam?

ARTIST.   All you need to do is die first. *(Lights down on artist, up on Suzy.)*

WILBUR.   *(Off-stage.)* Suzy, want to come out and play? It's not Wilbur.

SUZY.   (Sings.)
          DEAR JOHN I HAVE TO SAY
          YOUR LETTER CAME TODAY
          AND HEARING YOUR VOCATION TOOK MY
          BREATH AWAY

(Lights up on John, Reverend One [played by Barber] and Reverend Two [played by Bob].)

REVEREND ONE.   He wants to be a Reverend, Halleluia.

REVEREND TWO.   Say Halleluia!

JOHN.   Halleluia!

REVEREND ONE.   He wants to be baptized, Halleluia!

REVEREND TWO.   Say Halleluia!

JOHN.   I said it.

REVEREND ONE.   Johnny Pye, hold your nose for the Holy Dunk —

JOHN.   (Sings.)
          A PREACHER
          I WANT TO BE A PREACHER
          I THOUGHT IT WAS A DOCTOR
          AND THEN I THOUGHT IT WAS AN ARTIST
          BUT NOW I'VE GOT IT RIGHT
          SO NARROW MINDED
          AND BLINDED
          I'M DONE PRETENDING
          THE TRUE LIFE
          IS NEW LIFE
          THAT'S NEVER ENDING
          REVEREND PYE
          REVEREND PYE
          IN HIS HANDS
          WE WILL LIVE
          IN HIS HANDS
          WE WILL NEVER DIE
          NEVER DIE
          THERE BY THE GRACE OF GOD GO I
          THE RIGHT REVEREND
          JOHNNY

(Reverend One grabs John by neck, is about to dunk.)

REVEREND ONE.   JOHNNY PYE! I baptize you in the name of —

REVEREND TWO.   Hold on there! Are you baptizing the boy or bobbing for apples? You got to get him *all* wet —

REVEREND ONE.   You want to save him or drown him?

REVEREND TWO.   I want him baptized the right way —

REVEREND ONE.   You can't get righter —

REVEREND TWO.   You let go — (*Reverend Two pulls John up. They struggle, pulling John between them.*)

REVEREND ONE.   (*To John.*) I'll save you, Son. (*Third Reverend enters: Timmy Joe Jim. He prays at a distance. He is the Foolkiller.*)

REVEREND TWO.   I'll save you first!

JOHN.   Men — MEN! (*Points to Reverend Timmy Joe Jim.*) Who is that?

REVEREND ONE.   Why that's the Very Right Reverend Timmy Joe Jim! (*Crosses to him.*) Reverend Jim, this is an unexpected Honor!

JOHN.   It's him! It's the Foolkiller!

REVEREND TWO.   Reverend Pye!

JOHN.   It's you!

REVEREND JIM.   Who is this Man?

JOHN.   You know who I am! (*To Reverends One and Two.*) He's lying to you —

REVEREND ONE.   He's no one, Reverend; a *former* seminarian.

JOHN.   Get away from him! Don't you see who he is?

REVEREND TWO.   (*Reverend Two grabs John's arms.*) Son, let's you and me go pray real hard.

JOHN.   Let me go! You don't fool me, you never will! And you won't take me! Ever! (*John breaks away, runs out. Reverend Two follows him to make sure he's gone.*)

REVEREND ONE.   Reverend Jim, I apologize. I feel terrible about this, I truly do.

REVEREND JIM/FOOLKILLER.   Don't think twice about it. Why don't you sit down, Reverend? You don't look well. You don't look well at all. (*Foolkiller puts his hand on Reverend One's shoulder; sound of thunder crashing as Reverend One turns to face his death. Lights down on Foolkiller, Reverend One; lights up on the Captain [played by Bill]; he is nailing a recruitment poster to a tree. Another crash of thunder, Johnny Pye, jacket above his head, runs for shelter, stopping by the Captain.*)

CAPTAIN.   No sense running from a storm, son, it follows you.

JOHN.   I'm not.

CAPTAIN.   (*Smiles.*) Mrs. after you?

JOHN.   No; I'm not married. Not yet, anyway.

CAPTAIN.   (*Still nailing.*) Got a job?

JOHN.   Can't say I do. (*Captain steps aside; John looks at the poster. Captain takes a pad of paper from under his arm.*)

CAPTAIN.   Then I've got one for you, if you're man enough. Sign right here.

JOHN.   The army? Can't do it, Sir; not now anyway. I've got to go home, see my girl. Good luck to you — *(John puts coat up; he's about to run again.)*
CAPTAIN.   Afraid of getting killed? *(John looks at him.)* That's natural enough. But let me tell you something, son. You'll never really know what living is all about 'til you can face dying. *(Sound of thunder.)* We'd better get out from under this tree. Lightning's getting closer.
JOHN.   I'll sign that first. *(Captain hands John the pad; John signs. Lightning lights up the sky. Blackout. Lights up on Martinsville.)*
BARBER.   *(Off-stage.)* Get out and don't come back, you little weasel! *(Wilbur is thrown out from off stage, lands on the ground. Suzy Marsh is walking by.)*
SUZY.   Wilbur! What happened!
WILBUR.   Just quit my job. *(Yells back in wings.)* Hey; there's a reason they call it PETTY cash! *(Suzy starts to go.)* Suzy, the Optimist Club has their Tomato Stomp tonight. Want to go?
SUZY.   No thank you, Wilbur.
WILBUR.   And why not? You don't like to dance or you don't want to go with me?
SUZY.   I like to dance.
WILBUR.   Great! See you at seven! *(Suzy exits; sound of train whistle. Johnny Pye enters; he is dressed in a soldier's uniform from the Spanish American War.)* Johnny Pye!
JOHN.   Wilbur Wilberforce!
WILBUR.   Well well. This is a real surprise, isn't it? I mean, does anybody know you're back in town?
JOHN.   It's just a station stop; I wanted to surprise Suzy.
WILBUR.   Of all the days for her to go to Europe!
JOHN.   What?
WILBUR.   I put her on the train east this morning! She won't be back 'til at least ... *(Suzy enters, sees John.)*
SUZY.   John!
JOHN.   Suzy! *(They hug; Wilbur watches.)*
WILBUR.   Oh, *this* Suzy!
SUZY.   *(Breaks from hug.)* John, your uniform —
WILBUR.   I noticed that too ...
JOHN.   I joined the army —
WILBUR.   That's great. Guns, marching, make some buddies ...
JOHN.   We've got to win this war.
SUZY.   How long did you sign up for?
WILBUR.   Could make a career of the army —
SUZY.   Wilbur —

JOHN.   Could we have a little time alone?

WILBUR.   Fine with me, if Suzy won't mind ...

JOHN.   Wilbur —

WILBUR.   Just kidding! Soldier boy. *(Wilbur exits.)*

JOHN.   I don't have much time. We're shipping out of New York City.

SUZY.   I don't understand. *(Pause.)* When you wrote you said there was no sense running anymore, you were tired of it —

JOHN.   I am! This is different.

SUZY.   It is?

JOHN.   You know it is. This is something I have to do.

SUZY.   And after the war? What will the next something be?

JOHN.   Suzy —

SUZY.   You've made up your own mind, John, and you should. But you can't do it for both of us — not any more.

JOHN.   Suzy, you now how I feel about you.

SONG: GOODBYE JOHNNY (Reprise) (John and Suzy)

SUZY.   I'm not sure that I do. And I'm not sure that you do, either. *(Sound of train whistle.)*

JOHN.   *(Starts to exit, stops.)* Will you write me?

SUZY.   *(Sings.)*

    I GUESS THAT I WILL

    JOHN, YOU'VE MADE UP YOUR MIND WHAT YOUR LIFE

    IS TO BE

    BUT EACH STEP THAT YOU TAKE IS A STEP WITHOUT ME

    SO WE'LL LEAVE US AS PEN PALS AND LEAVE IT TO FATE

    I CAN PROMISE TO WRITE

    BUT I CAN'T PROMISE TO WAIT

JOHN.   *(Sings.)*

    SUZY MARSH

SUZY.   *(Sings.)*

    JOHNNY PYE

JOHN.   *(Sings.)*

    SUZY MARSH

(Barber, Bill and Bob enter as John and Suzy sing each other's names, anticipating their kiss. As they are about to connect, Wilbur runs in.)

WILBUR.   OH NO! The train's pulling out — *(John starts to leave, returns and kisses Suzy. Sound of a train whistle. John starts to leave again, the Barber calls to him.)*

BARBER.   Johnny? *(Barber, Bill and Bob salute John. Train whistle. John salutes and exits. Barber, Bill, Bob and Wilbur look to Suzy as she watches John go. Reassuring Suzy.)* He'll be back.

BILL.   You bet. *(Wilbur begins to approach Suzy, past Bob.)*

BOB.   Keep walkin', weasel. *(All men leave. We hear the train rolling out of the station.)*

SUZY.   *(Sings.)*
GOODBYE JOHNNY
JOHNNY GOODBYE
I'LL BE YOUR FRIEND
FROM HERE TO THE END
OF THE MOON AND THE SKY
SOME BY THEIR DREAMS ARE ALWAYS LED
AND SOME OF US STAY TO BUILD A LIFE INSTEAD

(As Suzy concludes, Wilbur enters, carrying mailbag.)

WILBUR.   Guess who's the new postmaster? *(Lights down on Suzy, Wilbur. In the dark, we hear the sounds of battle and see the flashes of explosions. Lights up on John and Captain, guns over the side of a trench. It is now 1945.)*

CAPTAIN.   They say these holes and mud hills used to be a farm.

JOHN.   How long do we wait here, Sir?

CAPTAIN.   'Til we get orders from the Colonel.

JOHN.   Maybe we should just charge them instead of hunkering down. *(Captain looks at John.)*

CAPTAIN.   How many men do we have here, Pye?

JOHN.   Close to fifteen hundred, Sir.

CAPTAIN.   That's close to fifteen hundred different ideas of what to do and when to do it. That's why we have Colonels, son. So only one man makes a fool of himself.

JOHN.   I guess.

CAPTAIN.   I got a special assignment for you, Pye. *(Takes out a letter.)* If anything happens to me, you make sure this letter gets to my wife.

JOHN.   Yes, Sir. *(Pause.)* I didn't know you had a wife, Sir.

CAPTAIN.   I'm not sure she'd agree I still do. We didn't leave on the best of terms, exactly.

JOHN.   Sir, could I ask you something? Did you ever wish you didn't get married?

CAPTAIN.   No more than a couple hundred times. On the whole, I'm glad I did. 'Course, I also enjoy the army. Not everybody's taste.

JOHN.   No, Sir.

CAPTAIN.   I'll tell you this, though. Living with any human being year after year is a tougher battle than taking any of these mud-hills. *(Pause.)* That what you really running from, Pye? *(John hears footsteps.)*

JOHN.   Sir, I hear something —

CAPTAIN.   What's that, John?

JOHN.   Footsteps. Can't you hear them?

CAPTAIN.   I don't hear a thing. *(Foolkiller emerges from the darkness behind them. John turns, points his gun at him and yells to the Captain.)*

JOHN.   Watch out! *(Captain turns, sees nothing. The Foolkiller shakes his head.)*

FOOLKILLER.   No, John.

CAPTAIN.   *(To John, annoyed.)* What in the name of — *(Sound of a shot; Captain collapses, shot in the back. Throughout the rest of the scene, scattered gunshot is constant.)*

JOHN.   You killed him!

FOOLKILLER.   No, a bullet did. I'm just here to collect. *(Foolkiller reaches down to the Captain.)*

JOHN.   *(Raising gun.)* Don't touch him or I'll shoot!

FOOLKILLER.   Stand aside, John.

JOHN.   Why are you doing this? Killing everyone around me?

FOOLKILLER.   John, this isn't personal. You recognize me. You're the only one who does. Most people can ignore me nearly all their lives.

JOHN.   I won't let you take him!

FOOLKILLER.   Now John ...

JOHN.   You'll have to take me, too.

FOOLKILLER.   That's very noble, but very foolish.

JOHN.   You told me once all men are fools; I guess I don't have much choice in the matter.

FOOLKILLER.   Maybe I can give you a choice, Johnny Pye. I'll tell you what: You tell me how a man can be a human being and not a fool, you tell me that, and I'll let you off permanent.

JOHN.   "A human being and not a fool?"

FOOLKILLER.   That's right.

JOHN.   And if I answer it —

FOOLKILLER.   You save yourself the cost of a tombstone. Think about it John. You've got plenty of time now. *(Sound of a shot: John drops to the ground. Foolkiller reaches down for the Captain.)* Sir, we need to be moving out. *(Lights down on Foolkiller, John and Captain. Lights up on Wilbur in the Martinsville post office. Stack of boxes and letters before him.. Wilbur takes up a box, reads marking.)*

WILBUR.   "To Constable Byrnes. Fragile." *(Wilbur shakes the box violently; we hear contents smashing, glass shattering.)* Yes indeed. *(Wilbur unwraps a brown paper parcel.)* Aha! More of those girlie magazines for Jimmy Dillingham. Well, trash does not circulate on this man's route. Hmm. Neville Pink got a letter from his mother. I wonder if she sent him that money he asked for. *(Opens letter, puts money in his pocket.)* Yup.

SONG: HANDLE WITH CARE (Wilbur)

WILBUR.   *(Sings.)*
>THERE'S A SECRET TO SUCCESS
>WHICH IS NONE OF YOUR DAMN BUSINESS
>ALWAYS SETTLING FOR LESS
>IS THE MODUS — OP — ER — EYE
>OF THE MASSES WHO DON'T PLOT
>THE UPSCALING OF THEIR LOT
>DOESN'T IT SEEM CLEAR
>DEDICATED PUBLIC SERVICE
>STARTS HERE
>THERE IS NO RIGHT PLACE
>THERE'S THIS PLACE
>THERE IS NO RIGHT TIME
>THERE'S NOW
>AND THE BREAK THAT YOU'VE BEEN WAITING FOR
>IS HERE AND NEVER YON
>BUT THE TRICK IS NOT TO GRAB IT
>TRUE ACHIEVEMENT IS TO NAB IT
>WITHOUT ANYONE SUSPECTING
>THAT IT'S GONE
>THAT'S WHY I

(Stamps packages violently. Throughout the rest of the song, he manhandles the mail as he sings of his "care.")
>HANDLE WITH CARE
>HANDLE WITH CARE
>EACH CATALOGUE COULD BE
>AN ORDER MEANT FOR ME
>A LITTLE GLUE A LITTLE STEAM
>A LITTLE RIP ALONG THE SEAM
>REMEMBER ALL IN LOVE AND WAR IS FAIR
>SO I TREAT YOUR MAIL LIKE IT WAS MY OWN

> I HANDLE WITH LOVE
> KID GLOVES
> AND CARE

(Opens letter. Lights up on Suzy, singing her words.)

SUZY.   *(Sings.)*

> DEAR JOHN

WILBUR. That's a promising start.

SUZY.   *(Sings.)*

> I CAN'T BEAR THIS TIME APART
> IF I'M NOT HERE WHEN YOU GET HOME
> I DIED OF A BROKEN HEART

WILBUR.   *(Sings.)*

> YOU LOVE A GIRL
> LIKE THIS GIRL
> YOU LOVE HER ALL YOUR LIFE
> AND YOU FIND THAT YOU ARE STANDING
> WITH HER HEART HELD IN YOUR HANDS
> AND THOUGH YOUR IMPULSE IS TO SHOOT IT
> YOU MUST CAREFULLY RE — ROUTE IT
> TRUE ROMANCE IS MORE CEREBRAL
> THAN YOUR GLANDS
> THAT'S WHY I

(Smashing more mail.)

> HANDLE WITH CARE
> HANDLE WITH CARE
> EACH ENVELOPE CONCEALS
> AFFAIRS AFFRONTS AND DEALS
> A LITTLE STEAM A LITTLE GLUE
> A LITTLE PEEK BY YOU KNOW WHO
> AND THEN I SEND IT OFF TO SPAIN
> OR LEAVE IT SOAKING IN THE RAIN
> AND IF YOU THINK THAT I'M GUILTY OF A CRIME
> REMEMBER ALL IN LOVE AND WAR IS FAIR
> SO I TREAT YOUR MAIL LIKE IT WAS MY OWN
> I HANDLE WITH FLARE
> HANDLE AND TEAR
> HANDLE WITH LOVE
> KID GLOVES

AND....

(Wilbur has picked up telegram. He stops suddenly, his expression changing. Shouts.)
Suzy! *(Lights up on Suzy, writing another letter. Wilbur runs to her.)* Suzy? I need to
see you —

SUZY.   Not now, Wilbur.

WILBUR.   We just got a telegram at the post office.

SUZY.   *(Pause.)* Wilbur? What happened?

WILBUR.   *(Pause.)* John's whole regiment, Suzy. All of them. *(Suzy throws her-
self into Wilbur's arms.)*

SUZY.   No! It can't be! *(Wilbur hugs her.)* Oh Wilbur ...

WILBUR.   I'm here, Suzy.. I'm right here. *(Suzy is in Wilbur's arms; Wilbur's con-
cern turns to bliss. Lights up in military hospital. John is in bed, eyes closed. A Nurse
[played by Mrs. Miller], Senator Marsh [played by Bob] and the President [played by Bill]
stop by John's bed. The Senator carries a box of medals.)*

PRESIDENT.   This boy's from your district, isn't he, Senator Marsh?

SENATOR.   Yes Sir, Mr. President.

NURSE.   The doctors don't think he has much of a chance, but he's a real
fighter. We have more soldiers in the West Wing, Mr. President.

PRESIDENT.   I'm sure you do.

SENATOR.   Sir, if you don't mind, I really need to catch a train.

PRESIDENT.   Come along, Senator. Leave the young man's medal here; he's
not going anywhere. *(The President puts the medal on bed. As they exit, Foolkiller appears.)*

FOOLKILLER.   "Not going anywhere." Did you hear that, John? *(John opens
his eyes, sings.)*

JOHN.   *(Sings.)*

  AT THE END OF THE ROAD
  AT THE END OF MY LIFE
  HE IS WAITING FOR ME
  WHY DID I RUN
  WHAT WAS THE PLAN
  I STOP AND LOOK AHEAD
  BUT I'M BACK WHERE I BEGAN
  AT THE END OF THE ROAD
  IS THERE A BEND TO THE ROAD
  DOES THE ROAD GO ON

FOOLKILLER.   Make up your mind, John, I can't wait all day. *(Sound of knock.
Lights up on Suzy, dressing for her wedding. Lights low on Foolkiller.)*

JOHN.   (*Thinking.*) Suzy.

WILBUR.   (*Off-stage.*) Suzy?

SUZY.   Not now, Wilbur. Oh, John. (*John sits up on bed.*)

JOHN.   (*Sings.*)

    AT THE END OF THE ROAD

SUZY.   (*Sings.*)

    AT THE END OF THE AISLE

JOHN.   (*Sings.*)

    HE IS WAITING FOR ME

SUZY.   (*Sings.*)

    HE IS WAITING FOR ME

JOHN and SUZY.   (*Sing.*)

    WHAT WILL I DO

JOHN.   (*Sings.*)

    HOW CAN IT BE

    THAT ALL I'VE LEFT BEHIND ARE SOME NAMES

    CARVED ON A TREE

SUZY.   (*Sings.*)

    AT THE END OF THE ROAD

    THERE'S NO BEND TO THE ROAD

    AND THE ROAD GO ON

JOHN.   (*Sings.*)

    I MUST GO ON

SUZY   (*Sings.*)

    AND ON AND ON

JOHN.   (*Sings.*)

    I MUST GO ON

SUZY.   (*Sings.*)

    AND ON AND ON

(*Nurse enters, sees John stirring.*)

NURSE.   Doctor! Come quickly! (*The Doctor runs in, his back to the audience, working over John. Music builds, Doctor turns, we see he is the Foolkiller.*)

FOOLKILLER.   You know, he just might make it. (*As figures clear, John jumps out of bed.*)

JOHN.   (*Sings.*)

    SUZY

    I'VE BEEN RUNNING A RACE

    BUT I SUDDENLY SEE

    THAT IF YOU'RE NOT WITH ME

I'M JUST RUNNING IN PLACE
SUZY

ANY FOOL SHOULD HAVE KNOWN
IT DOESN'T MATTER THE DISTANCE YOU'VE RUN
WHEN YOU REALIZE THE MOMENT YOU'RE DONE
YOU'RE ALONE

SUZY.   (Sings.)
JOHNNY

(John dresses hurriedly, Suzy puts on her veil. Lights up on Foolkiller, watching both of them.)

FOOLKILLER.   (Sings.)
EVERY SPARK OF THE WHEEL
LINGERS BRIGHT IN THE AIR
'TIL IT TUMBLES TO GROUND
AND GROWS DARK

BUT THERE'S ONLY ONE SPARK
THAT CAN BURN BRIGHTER
THAN THE FIRE FROM OFF OF MY WHEEL
THAT'S THE SPARK
THAT A HEART CAN FEEL

JOHN.   (Sings.)
SUZY

(Sound of knock on Suzy's door.)

WILBUR.   (Sings.)
SUZY

SUZY.   (Sings.)
AT THE END OF THE AISLE
HE IS WAITING FOR ME

JOHN.   (Sings.)
AT THE END OF THE ROAD
SHE IS WAITING FOR ME

(Suzy calls down to Wilbur.)

SUZY.   Now, Wilbur. (Suzy slowly crosses to an awaiting Wilbur.)

JOHN.   (Sings.)
I'VE BEEN
RUNNING ALONE
ALL OF MY LIFE

ALWAYS AFRAID THAT THE END WOULD APPEAR
RUNNING ALONE
WASTING MY LIFE
BUT TODAY I FINALLY SEE THERE IS NOTHING LEFT
TO FEAR
IF AT THE END OF THE ROAD
THERE'S A FRIEND IN THE ROAD

JOHN and WILBUR.   *(Sing.)*
    SUZY

(Suzy takes Wilbur's arm.)

SUZY.   *(Sings.)*
    AND THE ROAD GOES ON

WILBUR.   *(Sings.)*
    AND THE ROAD GOES ON

JOHN.   *(Sings.)*
    AND THE ROAD GOES —

(Nurse has run back in at song's conclusion; with her is the President and the Senator.)

NURSE.   Young man, get back in that bed!

JOHN.   I'm going back to Martinsville and nothing's going to stop me!

SENATOR.   Not before you get a handshake and a medal from the President.

JOHN.   Mr. President! Sir!

PRESIDENT.   Martinsville, did you say? *(Takes out letter from coat.)* I just signed a Federal Warrant to arrest a man from Martinsville on mail fraud, a Wilbur Wilberforce —

JOHN.   WILBUR WILBERFORCE!

SENATOR.   That can't be! Why, he and my niece Suzy Marsh —

JOHN.   SUZY MARSH!

PRESIDENT.   *(To John.)* Suzy Marsh?

SENATOR.   *(Looks at watch.)* They're about to be —

JOHN.   DON'T SAY IT! *(Sound of wedding march being played, blackout on men, lights up on Wilbur Wilberforce, aged minister [played by Bill] and guests. Minister is nearly blind.)*

MINISTER.   Do you take this —

WILBUR.   Not yet; she's not here yet.

MINISTER.   Tell her to hurry up; I got a funeral coming in. *(Suzy Marsh walks up the aisle.)*

WILBUR.   *(To Minister.)* Now.

MINISTER.   Do you — *(Johnny Pye runs in, stands at church door.)*

JOHN.   Suzy Marsh!

MINISTER.   Take this man —

SUZY.   Johnny Pye!

MINISTER.   To love, honor ...

WILBUR.   Wait a minute, he's dead!

MINISTER.   Then he's gotta wait for the funeral! *(John runs up the aisle to Suzy.)*

SUZY.   John, you're alive!

JOHN.   Suzy, you look so —

SUZY.   So do you, John — *(John is about to embrace her, but Suzy pulls back, suddenly enraged.)* Where have you been?

JOHN.   I wrote you, you never answered —

SUZY.   I never stopped writing, you did.

WILBUR.   *(Nudging Minister.)* START, START.

MINISTER.   Do you, Suzy Marsh, take this man — *(To Wilbur.)* Who is he?

WILBUR.   *(Venomous.)* Johnny Pye.

MINISTER.   To love, honor and obey through ... *(Voice trails off, John speaks over him.)* ... better or worse, sickness and health, in richness and poorness ...

JOHN.   I know you said you wouldn't wait, Suzy. But do you ever think of me?

MINISTER.   ... 'Til death do you part?

SUZY.   I do.

MINISTER.   And you, Johnny Pye ...

WILBUR.   Wilbur Wilberforce!

MINISTER.   ... Take this woman, Suzy Marsh ... *(Repeats invocation as before.)*

SUZY.   And you, John? What about you? Did you remember me now and again?

MINISTER.   ... 'Til death do you part?

JOHN.   I do, Suzy. *(Walks toward her.)* Always.

MINISTER.   I now pronounce you Johnny Pye and you Suzy Marsh man and wife.

WILBUR.   That's my wife! She's mine! He hasn't even had a blood test!

MINISTER.   You may now kiss the bride. *(John and Suzy kiss; congregation cheers and throws rice.)*

WILBUR.   That's my kiss! That's my rice! *(Senator runs in.)*

SENATOR.   Wilbur Wilberforce?

WILBUR.   Senator Marsh!

SENATOR.   You're under arrest!

WILBUR.   I never touched those letters! *(Pause.)* Oops.

MINISTER.   Quiet, you weasel! *(Old Minister drags Wilbur out.)*

SENATOR.   Congratulations, Mr. Pye! You are hereby appointed by the President of the United States Postmaster of Martinsville! *(Wedding bells; crowd cheers and disperses, leaving John and Suzy alone. Their excitement turns into nervousness.)*

JOHN.   *(Pause.)* Nice dress.

SUZY.   Thanks.

JOHN.   *(Pause.)* Should we be going on a honeymoon or...?

SUZY.   Well ...

JOHN.   Where were you and...?

SUZY.   *(Quickly.)* Niagara Falls. Wilbur said he won the tickets in the mail.

JOHN.   Nice place, Niagara Falls.

SUZY.   You've been there?

JOHN.   Uh-huh. *(Pause.)* If you like Falls, they got 'em.

SUZY.   We don't have to go there. We don't have to go anywhere. I guess you'd like to stay in one place for a while *(Pause.)* Wouldn't you?

JOHN.   Sure. *(Pause.)* Looks like Martinsville hasn't changed much.

SUZY.   No. I guess not.

JOHN.   No. *(Pause.)* Not much at all.

SONG: CHALLENGE TO LOVE (Suzy, John, Company)

SUZY.   *(Sings.)*
    A HICK LITTLE TOWN
    WITH A LITTLE OLD MAID
    STUCK AND SETTLING DOWN
    WITH THE SAME LIFE HE'D HAVE IF HE STAYED

JOHN.   So we're married.

SUZY.   We're married all right.

JOHN.   *(Sings.)*
    I'LL NEVER LIVE UP TO THE MAN IN HER MIND
    WHEN SHE WAKES FROM THIS DREAM SHE'LL LOOK UP AND
    SHE'LL FIND I'M THE

SUZY.   You look the same, John.

JOHN.   *(Sings.)*
    I'M THE SAME

SUZY.   I think you got even taller.

JOHN.   You got pretty big yourself. In a *good* way!

SUZY.   *(Sings.)*
    HE THINKS THAT I'M FAT

JOHN.   *(Sings.)*
         SHE MUST THINK I'M A FOOL

SUZY.   *(Sings.)*
         AND I DON'T EVEN KNOW HIM

JOHN.   *(Sings.)*
         I DON'T EVEN KNOW HER

SUZY.   *(Sings.)*
         IT'S NOT GOING TO WORK

JOHN.   *(Sings.)*
         THIS COULD BE A MISTAKE

SUZY.   *(Sings.)*
         I SHOULD TELL HIM RIGHT NOW

JOHN.   *(Sings.)*
         I SHOULD TELL HER RIGHT NOW

So ...

SUZY.   So ...

JOHN.   *(Sings.)*
         SUZY

SUZY.   *(Sings.)*
         JOHNNY

(Behind them, Young Johnny and Young Suzy emerge, a memory, standing at the tree they once parted from.)

YOUNG JOHNNY.   *(Sings.)*
         SUZY

YOUNG SUZY.   *(Sings.)*
         JOHNNY

(Young Johnny begins to carve in tree.)

YOUNG JOHNNY.   I've gotta come back now. The tree says so.

JOHN.   *(Sings.)*
         THE UNFAMILIAR FACES

SUZY.   *(Sings.)*
         YOU'VE SEEN SO MANY PLACES

JOHN.   *(Sings.)*
         SO MANY PACES I HAVE RUN
         NOW THE RACES MAY BE OVER
         BUT THE JOURNEY

SUZY.   *(Sings.)*
         YES THE JOURNEY

BOTH.   (Sing.)
            NOW THE JOURNEY HAS BEGUN
            THE CHALLENGE TO LOVE
            FROM THE DISTANCE
            THROUGH A MEMORY
            IS A SHORT ROAD
            LEADING NOWHERE
            BUT THE CHALLENGE TO LOVE
            FACE TO FACE
            DAY BY DAY
            HEART TO HEART
            YEAR TO YEAR
            IS A LONG ROAD LEADING EVERYWHERE
            THOUGH IT'S HARD TO BEAR
            BECAUSE THE HARDEST THING IN LIFE TO SHARE
            IS LIFE

(Townspeople enter. John and Suzy exchange rings.)

TOWNSPEOPLE.   (Sing.)   JOHN.   (Sings.)
            LIFE GOES ROUND IN A CIRCLE
            GROWING YOUNG TO OLD AND
                TO YOUNG AGAIN   GOES ROUND
            NEVER SLOWING   AND ROUND
            GOING ROUND AND ROUND   AND ROUND
            BUT THEN ONCE YOU'VE GONE   ONCE YOU'VE
                                                       GONE

            YOU COME HOME AGAIN   YOU COME HOME
            YOU COME HOME LIKE JOHN   AGAIN

ALL.   (Sing.)
            THE CHALLENGE TO LOVE
            FROM A DISTANCE
            THROUGH A MEMORY
            IS A SHORT ROAD
            LEADING NOWHERE
            BUT THE CHALLENGE TO LOVE
            FACE TO FACE
            DAY BY DAY
            HEART TO HEART
            YEAR TO YEAR
            IS A LONG ROAD LEADING EVERYWHERE

            THOUGH IT'S HARD TO BEAR
            BECAUSE THE HARDEST THING IN LIFE TO SHARE
JOHN and SUZY.   *(Sing.)*
            IS LIFE.
(Foolkiller appears.)
SUZY.   Welcome home, John. *(Townspeople cheer and disperse; John and Suzy start to exit.)*
FOOLKILLER.   That's right, John. Welcome home. *(John hesitates. Thinking he heard something, he looks back over his shoulder. As music ends, Suzy turns John's head back in her direction, as if for a kiss.)*

BLACKOUT

ACT TWO

Lights rise on Barbershop. Time has passed. We are now in the late 1940s.

SONG: THE BARBERSHOP (Barber, Bill, Bob)

BARBER.   *(Sings.)*
    SNIP SNIP SNIP SNIP
    CLIP CLIP CLIP CLIP
    TRIM TRIM TRIM TRIM
    FIRST YOU NEXT HIM
    WORK WORK WORK WORK
    ALL DAY LONG I
    WORK AND SNIP AND CLIP AND TRIM

(Bill is in the chair for his haircut.)

BILL.   *(Sings.)*
    WE ROCK AND WE ROCK AND WE ROCK AND WE ROCK
    AND WE ROCK AND WE ROCK AND WE SIT IN A CHAIR
    AND WE WATCH PEOPLE WALKING AND TALKING AND
    TALKING AND WALKING
    FROM THERE OVER HERE AND FROM HERE OVER THERE
    OUT OF THE BLUE
    QUICK AS A WINK
    WHAT DO THEY DO
    WHAT DO THEY THINK THINK THINK THINK

(Bob is in the chair for his haircut.)

BOB.   *(Sings.)*
    WE SIT AND THINK
    WE THINK AND SIT
    PHILOSOPHIZE FROM A BARBER CHAIR
    CONSIDER LOCKE
    REJECT VOLTAIRE
    YOU SURE TAKE STOCK
    IN WHAT THEY WROTE
    WITH A RAZOR AT YOUR THROAT

BILL.   *(Sings.)*
> WE ROCK AND WE ROCK AND WE ROCK AND WE ROCK

BILL, BOB and BARBER.   *(Sing.)*
> AND WE ROCK AND WE ROCK AND WE SIT IN A CHAIR
> AND WE ROCK ROCK ROCK ROCK
> WORK WORK WORK WORK
> WATCH WATCH WATCH WATCH
> THINK THINK THINK
>
> YEAR AFTER YEAR AS WE SIT RIGHT HERE
> 'TWEEN THE RAZOR AND THE STROP
> WE BECOME MORE AWARE OF THE WORLD OUT THERE
> OUT IN FRONT OF THE BARBERSHOP
> AND SO ITS BACK, FORTH
> PERIPHERAL SIDE TO SIDE
> TWEEN THE SODA AND THE POP
> AND WE HEAVE A SIGH
> AS THE WORLD GOES BY
> IN FRONT OF THE BARBER
> FRONT OF THE BARBER
> FRONT OF THE BARBERSHOP
>
> SNIP SNIP SNIP SNIP
> CLIP CLIP CLIP CLIP
> TRIM TRIM TRIM TRIM
> WORK WORK WORK WORK

(We hear a dog barking. John enters, delivering mail, chased by off-stage dog. He comes into the barbershop.)

JOHN.   Boys.

BARBER.   How's married life, John?

BILL.   Don't see any chains on the boy yet.

JOHN.   *(Forces a smile.)* It's great. Just great.

BOB.   *(Pause.)* Uh-huh.

JOHN.   Tell me, I heard a riddle once. "How can a man be a human being and not a fool?" *(All three men regard John silently, puzzled.)*

BARBER.   Need a haircut, John?

JOHN.   I've gotta go. *(John exits, pause.)*

BILL.   "How can a man be a human being and not a fool."

BOB.   Think it's a trick question? *(Sound of a doorbell. Lights down on barbershop; up on John delivering mail to unseen customer.)*

JOHN.   Here you are, Flora Dell: milk bill and the *Home Journal.* And I've got a riddle for you: "How can a man be a human being and not a fool." *(Pause.)* No ma'am. It has nothing to do with the Barbershop. *(Lights down on John, up on barbershop.)*

ALL.   *(Sing.)*
WE ARE THREE
WE ARE ALWAYS THREE
FROM THE KINDERGARTEN YEARS
TRIPLE THREATS AND MUSKETEERS
OF THE AVENUE
ALWAYS YOU AND YOU AND ME

BARBER.   *(Sings.)*
ONE

BOB.   *(Sings.)*
TWO

BILL.   *(Sings.)*
THREE

ALL.   *(Sing.)*
YEAR AFTER YEAR AS WE SIT RIGHT HERE
'TWEEN THE WHISKER AND THE CHOP
SIR WE DON'T INTERFERE WITH THE WILD FRONTIER
OUT IN FRONT OF THE BARBERSHOP
AND SO IT'S SCRATCH, STRETCH
SPIT CAREFULLY TURN THE PAGE
'TWEEN THE SODA AND THE POP
AND WE CALMLY WAIT
LEAVING ALL TO FATE
RIGHT HERE IN THE BARBERSHOP
RIGHT HERE IN THE BARBERSHOP
RIGHT HERE IN THE BARBER HERE IN THE BARBER
HERE IN THE BARBERSHOP

BARBER.   *(Sings.)*
WORK WORK

BILL.   *(Sings.)*
ROCK ROCK

BOB.   (Sings.)
         THINK THINK
ALL.   (Sing.)
         YUP

(Lights down on barbershop; up on John and Suzy; they are standing over a basin, miming the washing of dishes, a window before them. Suzy washes, John dries.)

JOHN.   Missed a spot. (Suzy, angry, takes dish back from him.) Don't get upset about it.

SUZY.   Why would I be upset? Because the first thing you say to me all night is "Missed a spot?"

JOHN.   That's not true.

SUZY.   John, you're a million miles away.

JOHN.   That's ridiculous!

SUZY.   What did we eat for dinner?

JOHN.   (Pause.) You think I don't know that?

SUZY.   I know you don't.

JOHN.   We had ... leftovers.

SUZY.   Leftover what?

JOHN.   Leftovers! Leftover meat! Leftover vegetables!

SUZY.   I guess I was wrong.

JOHN.   That's right.

SUZY.   You weren't checking for spots, you were checking for clues.

JOHN.   Fine.

SUZY.   Fine. (Pause.) You didn't dry that one. (John picks up plate, shows it to Suzy, throws it out the window.)

JOHN.   It's dry now.

SUZY.   JOHN! What will the neighbors say!

JOHN.   You missed a spot!

SUZY.   That does it! (Suzy takes a plate, throws it out the window. Sound of a crash. John throws another. Sound of a crash. Suzy throws one more. No crash. John watches, impressed.)

JOHN.   That really took off.

SUZY.   John!

JOHN.   It did. Took a bird down, too. A tree ... (Suzy can't restrain a smile. John sees it; they embrace.)

SUZY.   Oh John, I wish we were both a million miles away.

JOHN.   What?

SUZY.   After all the places you've been, how can you stand living in

Martinsville?

JOHN.   You're here.

SUZY.   I don't want to be. I can't bear one more day working at the grocers, watching everybody buy the same things, say the same things. John, I get so afraid one morning I'm going to get up and look in the mirror and say: Oh no, that's my mother. And I'll go through the whole rest of my life without getting excited about anything.

JOHN.   *(Pulls away.)* Let's get the suitcases.

SUZY.   What? Where will we go?

JOHN.   Anywhere you like.

SUZY.   What about our jobs?

JOHN.   Maybe they'll be here when we come back, and maybe we won't come back at all.

SUZY.   Yes! *(Suzy kisses John passionately. They get more and more excited.)* Let's go somewhere neither of us has ever been. Just pick a spot on the map.

JOHN.   Sounds good to me.

SUZY.   Maybe we should throw away the map.

JOHN.   Even better.

SUZY.   We'll go as far as we can. *(They kiss again.)*

JOHN.   Let's go.

SUZY.   Tomorrow morning. *(Suzy leads John off stage. Takes a gravyboat, tosses it out the window, they go off. Lights down then up on Barber, Bill and Bob. Time has passed.)*

BARBER.   Hear John and Suzy are gonna have themselves a little Pye.

BILL.   Didn't take those two long, when you think about it.

BOB.   Not when you think about it. *(Pause.)*

BARBER.   I hear Flora Dell Drumminy stopped seeing Neville Pink.

BILL.   *(Pause.)* Don't care a lick what Neville Pink says about her new teeth. They look fine to me.

BARBER.   Sure do.

BOB.   Real fine.

BARBER.   And strong, too.

BILL.   Whale bone.

BOB.   Bet she could bite through barbed wire.

BARBER.   You think Neville's lips are healing up any?

BILL.   He can't say. *(Lights down on Barber, Bill and Bob, up on John and Suzy, 1948.)*

SONG: UNDERNEATH THE HOLLY TREE (John, Suzy, Company)

JOHN and SUZY.   *(Sing.)*
UNDERNEATH THE HOLLY TREE
STANDING MATRIMONIALLY
EVERY MOMENT SEEMS TO BE
BRAND NEW
FOR TWO
SUZY.   *(Sings.)*
TIME THAT WE GREW UP INSTEAD
OF SPENDING EVERY DAY IN BED
BOTH.   *(Sing.)*
TIME TO LOOK AND PLAN AHEAD
JOHN.   *(Sings.)*
THERE'S MORE IN STORE
BOTH.   *(Sing.)*
MARRIED WITH CHILDREN
SUZY.   *(Sings.)*
BURN THE CASSEROLE,
JOHN.   *(Sings.)*
JOIN THE PTA
BOTH.   *(Sing.)*
MARRIED WITH CHILDREN ON THE WAY
UNDERNEATH THE HOLLY TREE
ME AND YOU AND IT MAKES THREE
IF THE ROAD IS BUMPY WE
WON'T POUT
(Mrs. Miller enters.)
SUZY.   Look out!
BOTH.   *(Sing.)*
UNDERNEATH THE HOLLY
LIFE IS KINDA JOLLY
UNDERNEATH THE HOLLY TREE
UNDERNEATH THE HOLLY
NEVER MELANCHOLY
UNDERNEATH THE HOLLY TREE
(Lights up on Townspeople.)

TOWNSPEOPLE.   (Sing.)

> MARTINSVILLE SITS ON
>> THE WABASH
> EVER SINCE THE FLOOD
> FAMOUS FOR OUR MUD
> HOME OF FAMOUS WORLD EXPLORER
> LUMINARY, MAIL RESTORER
> JOHNNY PYE JOHNNY PYE JOHNNY PYE
> SO I GUESS THAT I
> WOULD AGREE
> MARTINSVILLE IS GOOD ENOUGH FOR ME

JOHN and SUZY. (Sing.)

> MARTINSVILLE SITS
> ON THE WABASH
> FAMOUS FOR OUR
> MUD

(John and Suzy exit.)

(Lights down on Townspeople, up on John, standing before an imaginary cradle. Suzy enters.)

SUZY.   Did the baby ...

JOHN.   He's fine. I couldn't sleep.

SUZY.   Have you been having those dreams again?

JOHN.   Did you hear that?

SUZY.   John, he gurgled. Babies make noise once in awhile. See? He's smiling.

JOHN.   *(Pause.)* Do you ever worry we're going to be terrible parents?

SUZY.   I'd worry if we didn't worry about it.

JOHN.   Look at his fingers curled up like that. I could watch him all night.

SUZY.   Good. *(She kisses him.)* You have the three o'clock bottle. *(Lights down on John and Suzy. As lights come up, Wilbur runs in, carrying a file, a ball and a chain on his leg. We hear bloodhounds baying in the distance.)*

WILBUR.   *(Sings.)*

> I REMEMBER MARTINSVILLE
> NEVER BEEN A TOWN MORE BORING
> DON'T TELL ME 'BOUT MARTINSVILLE
> WHERE THE LOCAL SPORT IS SNORING
> COULDN'T WAIT TO BREAK OUT
> SO I TRY TO MAKE OUT WHY
> I THIINK ABOUT IT MORE AND MORE EACH DAY
> MEMORIES OF MARTINSVILLE

(Takes out file.)

> I FILE

(Files in time to music.)

> AWAY

(Lights down on Wilbur, up on barbershop. Time has passed; it is 1949.)

BARBER.   Hear that weasel Wilberforce got himself out of jail.

BILL.   Hear he got into politics.

BOB.   Uh-huh.

BARBER.   Hear John and Suzy had themselves another little Pye.

BILL.   Those two are frisky, all right.

BOB.   Think I might go calling on Flora Dell. Now that she got use of her arm again.

BILL.   Fine looking woman, that Flora Dell.

BOB.   Sure is.

BARBER.   Real fine. Still, nobody should comb their hair in front of a thresher.

BILL.   Nope.

BOB.   No, Sir. *(Pause.)* Truth is, though, a hand don't need much more than three fingers anyhow. *(Lights down on barbershop; up on John and Suzy. John carries a bundled baby, Suzy is pregnant again.)*

JOHN and SUZY.   *(Sing.)*
> UNDERNEATH THE HOLLY TREE
> BOUNCING BABY ON OUR KNEE
> JUMPING UP IN JUBILEE
> FOR ONE, OUR SON

SUZY.   *(Sings.)*
> LOOK AT HOW HIS BLUE EYES SHINE

JOHN.   *(Sings.)*
> HE'S A GENIUS, THAT'S A SIGN

BOTH.   *(Sing.)*
> EVEN LIKE TO HEAR HIM WHINE

SUZY.   *(Sings.)*
> YOU BET

JOHN.   *(Sings.)*
> HE'S WET

(Lights up on Townspeople.)

ALL.   *(Sing.)*
> MARRIED WITH CHILDREN

JOHN.   *(Sings.)*
> WEDNESDAY CUB SCOUTS

SUZY.   *(Sings.)*
> THURSDAY NIGHT'S BALLET

ALL.   (Sing.)

MARRIED WITH CHILDREN ON THE WAY

JOHN and SUZY.   (Sing.)

CHILDREN THINK THAT LIFE IS FREE

WISH WE HAD A WARRANTEE

LIFE WOULD BE A SHOPPING SPREE

IF SO

BUT NO

CHORUS.   (Sings.)

CHILDREN THINK

THAT LIFE'S FREE

WE'D NEED A

WARRANTEE

IF SO

BUT NO

ALL.   (Sing.)

BABY WANTS A DOLLY

BUY THE BOY A COLLIE

UNDERNEATH THE HOLLY TREE

UNDERNEATH THE HOLLY

LIFE IS KINDA JOLLY

UNDERNEATH THE HOLLY TREE

(Lights up on Foolkiller watching John Jr. [played by Young Johnny] play with John, his father.)

FOOLKILLER.   (Sings.)

FUNNY HOW IT SEEMS ALL THE DREAMS THAT YOU HAD

ONCE BELONGED TO YOUR DAD

AND THE DAYS YOU TOOK FOR GRANTED

SEEM AS SHORT AS SEEDS YOU PLANTED

LONG AGO

BUT THEY GROW

EVEN SO

THEN YOU KNOW

YOU'D BE CONTENT TO BE

A BRANCH THAT HOLDS A CHILD'S SWING

ON THE FAMILY TREE

(Lights up on barbershop; more time has passed.)

BARBER.   Hear Wilbur Wilberforce got as far as Congress before he got locked up again.

BILL.   Yep.

BOB.   Uh-huh.

BILL.   Hear Flora Dell's going to that Sadie Hawkins Dance all by her lonesome.

BARBER.   No way you'd catch me at such a darn fool dance. No, Sir.

BOB.   No how.

BILL.   *(Pause.)* So she didn't ask you, either?

BARBER and BOB.   Nope. *(Lights up on John, Suzy, John Jr. [played by Young Johnny] and Suzy Jr. [played by Young Suzy]. Suzy carries a bundled baby and is pregnant again. The kids are fighting. It is 1958.)*

ALL.   *(Sing.)*

    MARRIED WITH CHILDREN.

JOHN and SUZY.   *(Sing.)*

    NOT A MOMENT'S REST

    THAT'S THE PRICE YOU PAY

ALL.   *(Sing.)*

    MARRIED WITH CHILDREN IN THE WAY

(The family gets out of the car; the kids are still fighting.)

JOHN and SUZY.	CHORUS. *(Sing.)*
RAISING A FAMILY	RAISING UP
UNDERNEATH THE HOLLY TREE	A FAMILY
GUESS WE SHOULD HAVE	
STOPPED AT THREE	GUESS THEY
	SHOULD HAVE
WE SWORE	STOPPED THEY
	SWORE
NO MORE	NO MORE

(John and Suzy separate kids; Suzy exits with Suzy Jr.; John and John Jr. cross to bedroom where John Jr. gets ready for bed; Suzy returns to tuck John Jr. in.)

ALL.   *(Sing.)*

    UNDERNEATH THE HOLLY

    LIFE IS KIND OF JOLLY

    UNDERNEATH THE HOLLY TREE

    UNDERNEATH THE HOLLY

    FOOLS CONTENT WITH FOLLY

    UNDERNEATH THE HOLLY

    NEVER MELANCHOLY

    USUALLY VERY SILLY

    SHUCKS BY GOSH AND GOLLY

JOHN and SUZY.   *(Sing.)*

    WE ARE REALLY VERY HAPPY

    UNDERNEATH THE VERY SAPPY

    HOLLY TREE

ALL. *(Sing.)*
    MARTINSVILLE GROWS TREES AND CHILDREN
JOHN and SUZY. SHH!
BARBER. *(Sings.)*
    GOT NO WORMS AT ALL
(Blackout. In the darkness, the cry of John Jr. can be heard. Lights up as John and Suzy run to his bedside. Note: In the Lamb's production, the following scene and song included Suzy Jr. That version is included in the back of this playscript.)
JOHN JR. PA!
JOHN. *(Hugging John Jr..)* It's all right, bad dream? *(John Jr. nods; sound of young girl off stage [played by Young Suzy].)*
DAUGHTER. *(Off-stage.)* Mama!
SUZY. The girls are up; I'll settle them. *(Suzy exits, as.)* Hush now, pumpkins.
JOHN. You remember what the dream was?
JOHN JR. No.
JOHN. Well, I'm here now. Everything's all right.
JOHN JR. Pa? I don't want to go tomorrow.
JOHN. Fishing?
JOHN JR. I don't want to go out with the guys in the boat.
JOHN. Then you won't go. That's all there is to it.
JOHN JR. The other kids'll call me a sissy.
JOHN. Hmm. Maybe I won't let you go. Maybe you'll have to help me finish painting the house.
JOHN JR. Yeah?
JOHN. Sure could use a hand.
JOHN JR. I know the lake's not that deep. And I know I can swim.
JOHN. Better than anybody in the family. Better than me; that's for sure.
JOHN JR. Nah.
JOHN. Oh yes.
JOHN JR. I don't think about that in the rowboat. All I can think about is the water all around, and the land so far away I feel ... homesick or something.
JOHN. Well, I know what it feels like to be afraid of something. *(Pause.)* Very afraid.
JOHN JR. You do?
JOHN. Thing is, you have to fight back at it.
JOHN JR. How?
JOHN. By not letting it stop you from doing whatever you really want to do. Or else you'd never do anything at all.

JOHN JR.   I guess that sounds right.

JOHN.   Sure it's right. Now if only it could make the bad dreams go away. *(John hugs John Jr.)* Get some sleep, partner.

JOHN JR.   Pa; I'll go fishing. I think I should.

JOHN.   You bring home dinner, o.k.?

SONG: THE LAND WHERE THERE IS NO DEATH (John and John Jr.)

JOHN JR.   *(Sings.)*
    PA
    WHY DO PEOPLE DIE
    EVER WONDER WHY
    PEOPLE DIE
    EVERY DAY
    I WONDER DOES IT HURT
    FOR A BODY WITH NO SOUL
    TO BE LOWERED IN A HOLE
    IN WHAT THEY CALL A CASKET
    COVERED UP WITH DIRT
    MAYBE WE SHOULD DIG ONE UP AND ASK IT

JOHN.   *(Sings.)*
    SOMEWHERE
    THERE MUST BE A PLACE
    A BEAUTIFUL LAND WHERE THE RAIN AND THE TREES
    AND THE SAND AND THE BREEZE IN YOUR FACE
    AND THE FLOWERS AND GRASS AND THE HOURS THAT PASS
    ARE FREE FROM PAIN AND FLOW LIKE BREATH
    A LAND WHERE THERE IS NO DEATH
    AN UNBELIEVABLE BEAUTEOUS AND LOVELY LAND
    WHERE PEOPLE NEVER DIE
    SOMEWHERE

JOHN JR.   *(Sings.)*
    PA
    MAYBE I SHOULD GO
    RUN AWAY AND MAYBE SO
    ALL THE DREAMS WOULD BE GONE

JOHN.   *(Sings.)*
    YOU COULDN'T RUN THAT FAR
    THAT'S THE ONE THING THAT I KNOW

                    THEY WOULD FOLLOW EVEN THOUGH
                    YOU COULD RUN FOREVER

JOHN JR.   *(Sings.)*
                    I'D MISS YOU VERY MUCH
                    SAY YOU'LL NEVER EVER LEAVE ME

JOHN.   *(Sings.)*
                    NEVER

JOHN JR.   *(Sings.)*
                    SOMEWHERE

JOHN.   *(Sings.)*
                    DYING'S JUST THE SAME AS LEAVING
                    WHEN YOU'RE LEFT ALONE
                    LOTS OF PEOPLE END UP CRYING EITHER WAY
                    LEAVING MAY BE WORSE THAN DYING
                    WHEN YOU'RE OUT THERE ON YOUR OWN
                    SOMEWHERE
                    FAR AWAY

JOHN JR.   *(Sings.)*
                    SOMEWHERE

JOHN.   *(Sings.)*
                    SOMEWHERE

BOTH.   *(Sing.)*
                    THERE MUST BE A PLACE

JOHN.   *(Sings.)*
                    A BEAUTIFUL LAND WHERE THE PLAIN IS WIDE
                    AND THE WIND'S ON YOUR SIDE WHEN YOU RACE
                    NOT A CLOUD IN THE SKY AND THE FOLKS PASSING BY

BOTH.   *(Sing.)*
                    ARE FREE FROM PAIN AND FLOW LIKE BREATH
                    IN THE LAND WHERE THERE IS NO DEATH
                    AN UNBELIEVABLE BEAUTEOUS AND LOVELY
                    HAPPY AND WONDERFUL LAND
                    WHERE PEOPLE NEVER DIE

JOHN JR.   *(Sings.)*
                    NO ONE EVER DIES THERE

JOHN.   *(Sings.)*
                    NO ONE EVER DIES, SON
                    SO JOHNNY, DRY YOUR EYES

(John tucks John Jr.; shower of sparks can be seen in distance behind them. Lights down on John and John Jr., up on barbershop; Barber, Bill and Bob are still.)

BARBER.   Water wasn't even deep; they couldn't find him quick enough. They were playing and the boat tipped over. You know how boys are.

BILL.   Yep.

BOB.   Uh-huh.

BARBER.   Johnny loved that boy.

BILL.   He did.

BOB.   Yes he did. *(Lights down on barbershop, up on John, sitting on John Jr.'s bed, now empty. Suzy enters.)*

SUZY.   John, you've got to come out and see the children. *(John does not respond.)* John! *(Suzy exits, lights dim, John steps away for the bed; behind him the Foolkiller can be seen.)*

JOHN.   *YOU COWARD! WHERE ARE YOU? FACE ME LIKE A MAN, DAMN YOU!* Can't you do that? Were you afraid to take me, is that it? Take me now, take me instead.

FOOLKILLER.   It's not your time.

JOHN.   How could it be his? He was a little boy!

FOOLKILLER.   I never speculate. Don't have the imagination for it.

JOHN.   Would he have lived if I kept him home with me? Tell me that at least!

FOOLKILLER.   John, I know how you feel ...

JOHN.   You don't know! You don't feel anything!

FOOLKILLER.   *(Pause.)* All I can tell you is that time passes.

JOHN.   It will never cure the grief I have for my son.

FOOLKILLER.   Would you leave your wife a widow and your other children fatherless for the sake of your grief? *(John shakes his head "no.")* Go home to your family, John. Go home. *(John slowly walks off stage. As Foolkiller sings, we are at the funeral of John Jr. The family and town are there. John joins them, but can't bear to stay.)*

SONG: TIME PASSES   (Foolkiller, Company)

FOOLKILLER.   *(Sings.)*
    TIME PASSES
    NEVER NOTICE THAT IT'S NEAR
    TIME PASSES
    NEVER NOTICE THAT IT'S HERE
    TIME PASSES
    QUICK AND QUIET NOW IT'S GONE

TIME PASSES ON AND ON
THROUGH TIME
ALWAYS DUE OR FLED
SUDDENLY YOU FIND THERE IS MORE BEHIND
THAN THERE IS AHEAD

(Funeral disperses.)

BARBER, BILL, BOB and MRS. MILLER.   *(Sing.)*
TIME PASSES

FOOLKILLER.   *(Sings.)*
TOO BUSY TO THINK

BARBER, BILL, BOB and MRS. MILLER.   *(Sing.)*
TIME PASSES

FOOLKILLER.   *(Sings.)*
TOO BUSY TO FEEL

BARBER, BILL, BOB and MRS. MILLER.   *(Sing.)*
TIME PASSES

(Mrs. Miller exits.)

FOOLKILLER.   *(Sings.)*
TOO BUSY TO LAUGH, TOO BUSY TO KNEEL
HERE AND GONE AND ON AND ON AND ON
PAST

BARBER, BILL and BOB.   *(Sing.)*
TIME
TAKES A TOOTH, LEAVES A WRINKLE
TAKES A THOUGHT, LEAVES A MENTAL BLOCK
TAKES A HAIR, LEAVES AN EASY CHAIR TO ROCK AND
ROCK AND ROCK AND PASS THE TIME

(Suzy appears. Time has passed. Mrs. Miller passes by, older now.)

SUZY.   *(Sings.)*
TIME PASSES
TAKES THE PAIN AND LEAVES THE ACHE
TIME PASSES
TIME TO SLEEP AND TIME TO WAKE
TIME PASSES
ALL TOO SLOWLY
ALL TOO FAST
TIME TURNING FIRST TO LAST
IN TIME

TURNING BROWNS TO GREENS
SUDDENLY I'M TOLD
I AM GETTING OLD
TELL ME WHAT THAT MEANS

BARBER, BILL, and BOB.   *(Sing.)*
TIME PASSES.

FOOLKILLER.   *(Sings.)*
TIME PASSES

(John enters, pulls Suzy into another playing area. It is 1966.)

SUZY.   *(Laughing.)* Where are you taking me? *(Lights up reveal a picnic basket and cloth set up before the "tree"; John takes his hands off Suzy's eyes.)* A picnic!

JOHN.   See where we are?

SUZY.   Of course I do! Look at this tree! *(They look for the carving.)* Is it still there?

JOHN.   Right here — *(John looks.)* Oh no —

SUZY.   "John and Suzy *AND WILBUR?*" *(Suzy laughs; John joins in.)*

JOHN.   I don't know what's harder to believe; that we were ever that young or this old.

SUZY.   Forty-six isn't old. Once you get there.

JOHN.   Funny thing is, I feel the same. *(Pause.)* Never thought I'd be somebody's old man let alone somebody's grandpa.

SUZY.   You did a good job as an old man, old man.

JOHN.   You too, old lady. Happy anniversary. *(They kiss.)*

SUZY.   Happy anniversary.

JOHN.   Tell me something; are you happy?

SUZY.   Happy enough not to think about it.

JOHN.   *(Pause.)* I still miss him.

SUZY.   Of course you do.

JOHN.   *(Pause.)* I wasted so many years travelling; then I wasted a lot more hating as much as grieving. *(Pause.)* I don't want to waste any more of our time.

SUZY.   I love you, Johnny Pye.

JOHN.   I love you, too, Suzy Marsh.

SUZY.   *(Leans into him.)* So don't waste time. *(They kiss again. Lights down on John and Suzy, up on Foolkiller and Townspeople.)*

FOOLKILLER.   *(Sings.)*
AND IT SEEMS UNFAIR, UNKIND
WITH SO MUCH TO SPARE
WHEN YOU REALLY CARE
YOU FIND THAT TIME ISN'T THERE

TOWNSPEOPLE.   (Sing.)
        TIME PASSES TIME PASSES
FOOLKILLER.   (Sings.)
        AND IT TAKE SUCH TIME
        TO EXPLAIN THAT TIME
        ISN'T ALWAYS THERE
TOWNSPEOPLE.   (Sing.)
        TAKES THE SPRING, LEAVES THE SUMMER
        TAKES THE FALL, LEAVES THE WINTER SNOW
        TAKES THE SNOW, LEAVES THE GRASS TO GROW AND GROW
        AND GROW AND GROW
        AND PASS THE TIME
        PASS THE TIME
JOHN, SUZY and TOWNSPEOPLE.   (Sing.)
        TIME PASSES
        TAKES THE PAIN AND LEAVES THE ACHE
        TIME PASSES
        TIME TO SLEEP AND TIME TO WAKE
        TIME PASSES
        ALL TOO SLOWLY ALL TOO FAST
        TIME TURNING FIRST TO LAST
FOOLKILLER, JOHN, SUZY and TOWNSPEOPLE.   (Sing.)
        IN TIME
        TURNING BROWNS TO GREENS
        SUDDENLY I'M TOLD I AM GETTING OLD
        TELL ME WHAT THAT MEANS
        TIME PASSES
FOOLKILLER.   (Sings.)
        WINTER TO SPRING
TOWNSPEOPLE.   (Sing.)
        TIME PASSES
FOOLKILLER.   (Sings.)
        SUMMER TO FALL
TOWNSPEOPLE.   (Sing.)
        TIME PASSES
FOOLKILLER.   (Sings.)
        TIME
        AND IN THE END

THERE IS NO END
AT ALL

(Foolkiller checks his book, gestures to Mrs. Miller who joins him and slowly exits. Blackout. Lights up on barbershop, 1978.)

BARBER.   He's been asking everybody in town.

BOB.   *(Not hearing.)* Say again?

BILL.   He's been asking everybody that riddle again.

BARBER.   John's shook, that's why.

BOB.   He's shook, John is. With Suzy like she is.

BARBER.   Yep.

BILL.   Uh-huh. *(Lights up on John and Suzy; John sitting next to Suzy's bed, reading a newspaper to her.)*

JOHN.   Look at this now. Flora Dell's niece got voted Little Miss Martinsville.

SUZY.   All the Easter baskets are at the top of the hall closet. You've got to go downtown and get the candy.

JOHN.   *(Reading.)* Can't believe they want to call Martinsville a City. You call someplace a city and the first thing you know it starts filling up with people.

SUZY.   Make up the baskets, John. And not just for the grandkids; the big ones always say they don't want them, and pout if they don't get them. One big chocolate rabbit apiece, and spread around the jellybeans and malted eggs so they're even. Except for Katie. She's allergic to malted eggs, so give her extra jelly beans.

JOHN.   I hate those malted eggs. Things are so hard you could break your teeth on them.

SUZY.   You've got to do the baskets. *(Pause.)* No matter what.

JOHN.   Don't even know why they make malted eggs. They're like little rocks, little marbles somebody shellacked. Those green jellybeans aren't any better. Who eats green candy? *(Suzy gasps in pain.)*

SUZY.   Promise me, John.

JOHN.   I do, Suzy. I do.

SONG: CHALLENGE TO LOVE   (Reprise)

(Underscoring is heard; John and Suzy smile at each other.)

SUZY.   You remember ...

JOHN.   Uh-huh.

SUZY.   When I saw you run into the church ...

JOHN.   When I saw you ...

SUZY. *(Suzy smiles, sings.)*
  A HICK LITTLE TOWN
  WITH A LITTLE OLD MAID
  STUCK AND SETTLING DOWN
  IN THE SAME LIFE YOU'D HAVE IF YOU STAYED

JOHN. What a time that was. *(Sings.)*

SUZY. What a time.

JOHN. *(Sings.)*
  I'D NEVER LIVE UP TO THE MAN IN YOUR MIND
  SO AFRAID YOU'D WAKE UP AND YOU'D SUDDENLY FIND

SUZY. You're still the same, John. *(Suzy slowly crosses to John, sits on his lap.)*

BOTH. *(Sing.)*
  THE CHALLENGE OF LOVE
  FROM A DISTANCE
  THROUGH A MEMORY
  IS A SHORT ROAD
  LEADING NOWHERE
  BUT THE CHALLENGE TO LOVE
  FACE TO FACE
  DAY BY DAY
  HEART TO HEART
  YEAR TO YEAR
  IS A LONG ROAD LEADING EVERYWHERE
  THOUGH IT'S HARD TO BEAR
  BECAUSE THE HARDEST THING IN LIFE TO SHARE —

(Foolkiller appears.)

JOHN. GET AWAY FROM HER! SHE'S NOT GOING! YOU HEAR ME!

SUZY. John —

FOOLKILLER. She's in pain, John.

JOHN. I'm here, Suzy, I'm right here.

SUZY. Hold me —

JOHN. I'm holding you, Suzy.

SUZY. Tighter —

JOHN. I've got you, Suzy.

FOOLKILLER. Let her go, John.

JOHN. No ...

SUZY. *(In pain.)* John —

JOHN. I CAN'T!

FOOLKILLER.   Think of her, John. Think of her.

SUZY.   I'm so afraid.

FOOLKILLER.   Let me take her, John.

SUZY.   *(In pain.)* John!

JOHN.   It's all right, Suzy. It will be all right. You won't hurt anymore.

SUZY.   Oh John ...

JOHN.   I love you so much.

SUZY.   I love you best friend. *(Suzy looks at the Foolkiller and gives him her hand; Suzy slowly exits. As lights fade, John and Foolkiller exchange a look. Lights up on Grandchildren, Katie [played by Young Suzy] and Daniel [played by Young Johnny], both dressed in pajamas.)*

DANIEL.   I can't believe Dad and Mom are crying again.

KATIE.   Of course they are, silly.

DANIEL.   They keep saying it was all for the best, but they all keep crying.

KATIE.   I can't believe we're not gonna see Grandma again.

DANIEL.   *(Pause.)* Do you think we'll still get any Easter Candy?

KATIE.   Daniel Pye, you should be ashamed of yourself! Grandma's dead and all you can think about is candy?

DANIEL.   No!

KATIE.   Don't you care? Don't you care at all? *(Katie starts to cry, Daniel holds her.)*

DANIEL.   I do, Katie. I do. *(Knock on door; Katie sees someone enter over Daniel's shoulder.)*

KATIE.   Grandpa — *(John enters, holding two Easter baskets. He tries to smile.)*

JOHN.   Happy Easter, pumpkins. These are from Grandma. *(Lights down on John, Katie, Daniel; lights up on Barber, Bill and Bob, 1980.)*

BARBER.   Hear Johnny Pye shook hands with the President when he came to town.

BOB.   *(Long pause.)* What?

BARBER.   *(Shouting.)* Hear Johnny Pye shook hands with the President. That's two President's John shook. Fifty years apart.

BOB.   *(Pause.)* Shook hands with another one, too. What's his name, that old timer? *(Sounds of a jet fill the air; they look up, irritated.)*

BARBER.   You hear that?

BOB.   What?

BILL.   You hear that airplane?

BOB.   No. But look at that jet.

BARBER.   Don't know how they fly this low.

BILL.   Don't know how they fly this fast.

BOB.   Don't know how Flora Dell ever got her pilot's license. *(As they exit, lights change. John enters; he puts flowers on Suzy's grave. It is 1983. Wilbur Wilberforce enters, carrying a suitcase.)*

WILBUR.   Johnny Pye?

JOHN.   Wilbur? I thought you were still in prison.

WILBUR.   The warden let me out early. Christmas present.

JOHN.   Really.

WILBUR.   To the other prisoners. *(Pause.)* Heard about Suzy.

JOHN.   Almost five years now.

WILBUR.   Time sure ...

JOHN.   Don't it, though.

WILBUR.   I guess I ... I wanted to ... *(Wilbur can't get out the words of consolation. He reaches out for John's hand; the handshake becomes a hug. After a moment, both men pull back, embarrassed at the sentiment.)* So ...

JOHN.   Well ...

WILBUR.   You look old, Johnny Pye!

JOHN.   Look younger than you, Wilbur.

WILBUR.   I've seen barrels of prunes with less wrinkles.

JOHN.   And it looks like you ate every last one of them.

SONG: NEVER FELT BETTER (John, Wilbur, Company)

WILBUR.   *(Sings.)*
    I'VE NEVER BEEN LEANER

JOHN.   *(Sings.)*
    KEENER

WILBUR.   *(Sings.)*
    MEANER

BOTH.   *(Sing.)*
    NEVER FELT BETTER IN MY LIFE

JOHN.   *(Sings.)*
    I CAN STILL OUTRACE MY GRANDSON AND THE BOY IS
    NEARLY TWO

WILBUR.   *(Sings.)*
    I STILL HAVE A HEAD OF HAIR LEFT; WISH I HAD MORE
    TEETH TO CHEW
    AND I HEAR THAT I'M REGARDED BY SOME WIDOWS AS A
    ROUE

BOTH.   (Sing.)
         I NEVER FELT BETTER
JOHN.   (Sings.)
         SOUNDER
WILBUR.   (Sings.)
         ROUNDER
BOTH.   (Sing. Wilbur and John cross to opposite ends of the stage.)
         NEVER FELT BETTER IN MY LIFE
JOHN'S FAMILY.   (Off-stage.) Happy Birthday Dad/Grandpa!
LITTLE BOY.   (Played by Young Johnny.) Happy Birthday, Grandpa!
JOHN.   Why thank you, Daniel.
LITTLE BOY.   I'm Harley.
JOHN.   That's what I said. (Lights up on Wilbur and a Waitress [played by Mrs. Miller].)
WAITRESS.   One prune platter; that's two dollars even. Unless you get the Senior Citizen discount.
WILBUR.   (Offended.) Senior Citizen? Do I look like a Senior Citizen?
WAITRESS.   There's a twenty percent discount.
WILBUR.   Just call me Pops. (Wilbur sees John, hails him.) Johnny Pye!
JOHN.   Wilbur Wilberforce! (By their walks, voices, mannerisms, John and Wilbur age more at each meeting.)
WILBUR.   Long time no see!
JOHN.   Never long enough, Wilbur.
WILBUR.   You look awful.
JOHN.   Feel tip top. Saw you going into Dr. O'Rourke's office last week.
WILBUR.   (Covering.) That's right. Needed back ointment.
JOHN.   Oh?
WILBUR.   All the weight lifting.
(Sings.)
         I'VE NEVER FELT DANDIER
JOHN.   (Sings.)
         HANDIER
WILBUR.   (Sings.)
         RANDIER
BOTH.   (Sing.)
         NEVER FELT BETTER IN MY LIFE
WILBUR.   (Sings.)
         I CAN SHIMMY UP TO MIDNIGHT IF I TAKE A NAP ALL
         DAY

JOHN.   (Sings.)
        I CAN TEAR INTO A T BONE IF IT'S MASHED UP LIKE
        SOUFFLÈ
WILBUR.   (Sings.)
        CAN'T REMEMBER WHERE I'M GOING WHEN I'M GOING ALL
        THE WAY
BOTH.   (Sing.)
        OH I NEVER FELT BETTER
JOHN.   (Sings.)
        BUSIER
WILBUR.   (Sings.)
        DIZZIER
BOTH.   (Sing.)
        NEVER FELT BETTER IN MY LIFE
(Lights up on barbershop. Bill and Bob are aged. It is 1990. John joins them as they
are packing up the Barber's belongings. As they sing, the Foolkiller appears in the dis-
tance and is joined by the Barber, who looks back at the barbershop before he and the
Foolkiller exit.)
WILBUR, JOHN, BILL and BOB.   (Sing.)
        I REMEMBER YOUNGER DAYS ALL ASTIR
        RUNNING FAST AS I COULD GO ALL A BLUR
        BUT YOU KNOW
        NOW THAT I FINALLY SLOW
        SUCH AS IT SEEMS TO ME
        THERE SEEMS TO BE
        MUCH TO MUCH
        FOR THESE OLD EYES TO SEE
JOHN.   Fire!
MARGARET.   (Played by Young Suzy.) It's your birthday cake, Grandpa. (Lights
up on Wilbur, waking in a chair.)
NURSE.   (Played by Mrs. Miller.) Mr. Wilberforce, time for your medicine. (Nurse
walks by him; Wilbur leans over, slaps her behind.) Why did you do that?
WILBUR.   (Pause.) I don't remember. (Nurse exits; Wilbur and John walk C. Bob
joins them.)
BOB.   The sun sure don't heat like it used to.
JOHN.   Now the Fort Wayne Kekiongas, there was a baseball team.
WILBUR.   Did I ever tell you about the time ...
VOICES.   (All off-stage voices.) YES! (Bob wanders off; John sees Wilbur.)
JOHN.   Wilbur Wilberforce —

WILBUR.   Huh?

JOHN.   It's Johnny Pye!

WILBUR.   I knew that! Race you to the corner! *(They race, a desperate shuffle. Wilbur sees John winning, grabs at his chest.)* My heart!

JOHN.   *(Suspicious, but stops.)* It's on the other side of your chest!

WILBUR.   *(Chuckles, moves past John.)* I WON!

JOHN.   You old fool.

WILBUR.   *(Breathing heavy.)* Rather be an old fool than a dead fool.

JOHN.   What did you say?

WILBUR.   *(Sings.)*
    I NEVER FELT QUICKER

JOHN.   *(Sings.)*
    SLICKER

WILBUR   *(Sings.)*
    SICKER

(Both cough.)

BOTH.   *(Sing.)*
    NEVER FELT BETTER IN MY LIFE

JOHN.   *(Sings.)*
    I CALL ALL THE GRANDKIDS HONEY 'CAUSE I CAN'T TELL
    THEM APART

WILBUR.   *(Sings.)*
    I STILL DRESS MYSELF EACH MORNING, NEVER MIND I
    NEED A CHART

JOHN.   *(Sings.)*
    AND I STILL GET WHERE I'M GOING BUT I NEED A DAY'S
    HEAD START

BOTH.   *(Sing.)*
    OH I NEVER FELT BETTER

JOHN.   *(Sings.)*
    SPRYER

WILBUR.   *(Sings.)*
    LIAR

BOTH.   *(Sing.)*
    NEVER FELT BETTER IN MY LIFE
    NEVER FELT BETTER IN MY LIFE
    NEVER FELT BETTER IN MY
    NEVER FELT BETTER IN MY
    NEVER FELT BETTER IN MY

(Both gasp for air.)

NEVER FELT BETTER IN MY LIFE

(Lights change; Nurse comes for Wilbur, escorts him off stage. John stands C., thinking.)

JOHN.   "I'd rather be an old fool than a dead fool ..." *(Margaret enters [Young Suzy].)*

MARGARET.   Great Grandpa! Sit down! *(Leads John to chair.)*

JOHN.   I got it, Suzy. I finally got it —

MARGARET.   I'm Margaret, Great Grandpa. Do you need anything?

JOHN.   No, no. I'll just sit here awhile. You go play.

MARGARET.   I'll be in the kitchen, Great Grandpa. Call if you need me. *(Margaret exits.)*

JOHN.   *(Sings.)*

> AT THE END OF THE ROAD
> AT THE END OF MY LIFE
> WHAT IS WAITING FOR ME
> YOU KNOW YOU'RE A FOOL
> LIKE EVERY OTHER MAN
> WHEN YOU STOP TO LOOK AHEAD
> BUT YOU'RE BACK WHERE YOU BEGAN
> AT THE END OF THE ROAD
> THERE'S A BEND IN THE ROAD

(Lights up on Foolkiller. John rises, slowly crosses to him.)

So there you are.

FOOLKILLER.   Here I am.

JOHN.   I've been looking for you.

FOOLKILLER.   You've been looking for me? What can I do for you, John? *(Looks in book.)* No appointment I can see.

JOHN.   You asked me a riddle once. You remember?

FOOLKILLER.   I never thought you would.

JOHN.   "How can a man be a human being and not a fool."

FOOLKILLER.   And your answer?

JOHN.   When he's dead and buried.

FOOLKILLER.   That's right.

JOHN.   It is? That's what I've been trying to figure out all my life?

FOOLKILLER.   Simple enough. Tell me, John, does *knowing* it make you feel any wiser?

JOHN.   I can't say it does.

FOOLKILLER.   No answer will. It's the way you unravel it that makes one knot more interesting than the next. But you get what you've always wanted, Johnny

Pye. I'm letting you go. There'll be trouble in the office about it, but you've got to do what you like once in awhile.

JOHN.   Now slow down here. I figure as long as I answered it I deserve some choice in the matter.

FOOLKILLER.   What are you talking about now?

JOHN.   Take me with you.

FOOLKILLER.   Now? I can't do that.

JOHN.   I get what I want, you said that. Truth is, I'm an old man now.

FOOLKILLER.   John, I said you could live forever. You're passing up a valuable opportunity.

JOHN.   It would do wonders for the Martinsville Chamber of Commerce, I know that. 'Course, I would like to beat out Wilbur Wilberforce —

FOOLKILLER.   Can't issue a limited policy.

JOHN.   *(Pause.)* Tell me. About afterwards.... Are you likely to see your family again?

FOOLKILLER.   *(Pause.)* Can't tell you that. I only go so far.

JOHN.   Guess I'll take my chances. I'm no fool. *(John and Foolkiller sing.)*
(Sings.)
        AT THE END OF THE ROAD

FOOLKILLER.   *(Sings.)*
        AT THE END OF A LIFE

JOHN.   *(Sings.)*
        WHAT IS WAITING FOR ME

FOOLKILLER.   *(Sings.)*
        WAITING FOR YOU

JOHN.   *(Sings.)*
        HOW WILL I KNOW
        WHERE WILL I BE
        WHEN I TAKE THE FINAL STEP
        WHAT WILL BE AHEAD OF ME
        AT THE END OF THE ROAD

FOOLKILLER.   *(Sings.)*
        THERE'S A FRIEND IN THE ROAD

(Foolkiller has inscribed John's name in his book.)
Well, look at that; here's your name after all.

JOHN.   Thank you friend. *(Off-stage, Margaret's voice is heard.)*

MARGARET.   *(Off-stage.)* Great Grandpa! Talk to me!

JOHN.   There's Margaret coming for me. She'll take me back to the house.

FOOLKILLER.   Not this time —

FINALE: THE LAND WHERE THERE IS NO DEATH

(Foolkiller puts out hand; John gives Foolkiller his cane and hat. Music is heard; unseen Chorus. As Chorus sings, John feels younger and younger.)

BARBER, BOB:	SUZY, WILBUR, KIDS:	BILL, MRS. MILLER:	FOOLKILLER:
SOMEWHERE	SOMEWHERE	SOMEWHERE	
	GOODBYE, JOHNNY		
THE LAND WHERE	THE LAND WHERE	THE LAND WHERE	
THERE IS NO	THERE IS NO	THERE IS NO	
DEATH	DEATH	DEATH	
SOMEWHERE		SOMEWHERE	
THERE MUST BE	GOODBYE, JOHNNY		
A PLACE		SOMEWHERE	WATCH THE
			BLADE
			SCRAPE THE
			STONE
THE LAND WHERE	THE LAND WHERE		
THERE IS NO	THERE IS NO		
DEATH	DEATH		

ALL.   *(Sing.)*
    SOMEWHERE
    AN UNBELIEVABLE BEAUTEOUS AND LOVELY
    HAPPY AND WONDERFUL LAND

FOOLKILLER.   *(Sings.)*
    WHERE PEOPLE NEVER DIE

SUZY.   *(Off-stage. Sings.)*
    NO ONE EVER DIES JOHN

JOHN JR.   *(Off-stage sings.)*
    NO ONE EVER DIES, PA

(John Jr. runs on and into Johnny Pye's arms; Suzy appears; John and John Jr. join her.)

FOOLKILLER.   *(Sings.)*
    ANOTHER DAWN
    ANOTHER MORNING
    ANOTHER DAY

(John, Suzy and John Jr. exit as lights fade to black.)

THE END

ALTERNATIVE "LAND WHERE THERE IS NO DEATH" SCENE AND SONG, INCLUDING SUZY JR.

[From page 49]

JOHN.   ... Then you won't go. That's all there is to it. *(Suzy Jr. sneaks in.)*

JOHN. JR.   The other kids'll call me a sissy.

JOHN.   No they won't.

SUZY JR.   Sissy! Sissy!

JOHN JR.   Am not!

SUZY JR.   Are too!

JOHN.   All right! *(To Suzy Jr.) You* go back to bed!

SUZY JR.   But he's up!

JOHN.   Then be quiet. *(Suzy Jr. zips her lips up, gives John key.)* Well, maybe I won't let you go. Maybe you'll have to help me finish painting the house.

JOHN JR.   Yeah?

JOHN.   Sure could use a hand.

JOHN JR.   I know the lake's not that deep. And I know I can swim.

JOHN.   Better than anybody in the family. *(Suzy Jr. starts to protest; John gives her a look; she re-zips her lip, gives John key. To Suzy Jr.)* Right? *(Suzy Jr. nods with mouth zipped.)* Better than me; that's for sure.

JOHN JR.   Nah.

JOHN.   Oh yes.

JOHN JR.   I don't think about that in the rowboat. All I can think about is the water all around, and the land so far away I feel ... homesick or something.

JOHN.   Well, I know what it feels like to be afraid of something. *(Pause.)* Very afraid.

JOHN JR.   You do?

JOHN.   Thing is, you have to fight back at it.

JOHN JR.   How?

JOHN.   By not letting it stop you from doing whatever you really want to do. Or else you'd never do anything at all.

JOHN JR.   I guess that sounds right.

JOHN.   'Course it's right. Now if only it could make the bad dreams go away. *(John tucks John Jr. in and takes Suzy Jr.'s hand.)* Let's get some sleep.

SONG: THE LAND WHERE THERE IS NO DEATH

JOHN JR.   Pa; I'll go fishing. I think I should.

SUZY JR.   Yes! *(Looks at John, slaps her hand over her mouth.)*

JOHN JR.   *(Sings.)*

PA

WHY DO PEOPLE DIE

EVER WONDER WHY

PEOPLE DIE

EVERY DAY

I WONDER DOES IT HURT

FOR A BODY WITH NO SOUL

TO BE LOWERED IN A HOLE

IN WHAT THEY CALL A CASKET

COVERED UP WITH DIRT

SUZY JR.   *(Sings.)*

MAYBE WE SHOULD DIG ONE UP AND ASK IT

JOHN.   *(Sings.)*

SOMEWHERE

THERE MUST BE A PLACE

A BEAUTIFUL LAND WHERE THE RAIN AND THE TREES

AND THE SAND AND THE BREEZE IN YOUR FACE

AND THE FLOWERS AND GRASS AND THE HOURS THAT PASS

ARE FREE FROM PAIN AND FLOW LIKE BREATH

A LAND WHERE THERE IS NO DEATH

AN UNBELIEVABLE BEAUTEOUS AND LOVELY LAND

WHERE PEOPLE NEVER DIE

SOMEWHERE

JOHN JR.   *(Sings.)*

PA

MAYBE I SHOULD GO

RUN AWAY AND MAYBE SO

ALL THE DREAMS WOULD BE GONE

JOHN.   *(Sings.)*

YOU COULDN'T RUN THAT FAR

THAT'S THE ONE THING THAT I KNOW

THEY WOULD FOLLOW EVEN THOUGH

YOU COULD RUN FOREVER

SUZY JR.   *(Sings.)*

I'D MISS YOU VERY MUCH

(They look at her.)

SAY YOU'LL NEVER EVER LEAVE ME

JOHN and JOHN JR.   *(Sing.)*

NEVER

JOHN.   *(Sings.)*

DYING'S JUST THE SAME AS LEAVING

WHEN YOU'RE LEFT ALONE

LOTS OF PEOPLE END UP CRYING EITHER WAY

LEAVING MAY BE WORSE THAN DYING

WHEN YOU'RE OUT THERE ON YOUR OWN

SOMEWHERE

FAR AWAY

JOHN JR. and SUZY JR.   *(Sing.)*

SOMEWHERE

JOHN.   *(Sings.)*

SOMEWHERE

ALL THREE.   *(Sing.)*

THERE MUST BE A PLACE

JOHN.   *(Sings.)*

A BEAUTIFUL LAND WHERE THE PLAIN IS WIDE

AND THE WIND'S ON YOUR SIDE WHEN YOU RACE

NOT A CLOUD IN THE SKY AND THE FOLKS PASSING BY

ALL THREE.   *(Sing.)*

ARE FREE FROM PAIN AND FLOW LIKE BREATH

IN THE LAND WHERE THERE IS NO DEATH

AN UNBELIEVABLE BEAUTEOUS AND LOVELY

HAPPY AND WONDERFUL LAND

JOHN.   *(Sings.)*

WHERE PEOPLE NEVER DIE

SUZY JR.   *(Sings.)*

NO ONE EVER DIES THERE

JOHN JR.   *(Sings.)*

NO ONE EVER DIES, PA

(Suzy enters, spots Suzy Jr.)

SUZY.   You!

SUZY JR.   *(To John and John Jr.)* 'Night! *(She runs off, Suzy follows.)*

JOHN.   *(Sings.)*
    SO JOHNNY, DRY YOUR EYES.
(John tucks in John Jr. Blackout. Lights up on barbershop; Barber, Bill, Bob, are still.)
[Return to page 52)

PROPERTY LIST

ACT ONE

Locket (SUZY, YOUNG SUZY)
Appointment book with pen (FOOLKILLER)
Rag (FOOLKILLER)
Handkerchief (MR. WILBERFORCE)
Pocket watch (MR. WILBERFORCE)
Small brown cap (YOUNG JOHNNY)
Purse (MRS. MILLER)
1928 newspaper (MR. WILBERFORCE)
Barber cloth (BARBER)
Small white hand towel (BARBER)
Grinding wheel unit with stool (FOOLKILLER)
Large knife (FOOLKILLER)
Whittling knife (BILL)
Whittling wood (BILL)
Brush (BARBER)
Mug with shaving cream (BARBER)
Straight razor (BARBER)
Book, Paine's *Common Sense*
Ball (YOUNG SUZY, YOUNG JOHNNY)
Blanket for John Sr. (MRS. MILLER)
Pillow for John Sr. (MRS. MILLER)
Small sample case (MR. WILBERFORCE)
Hobo stick (YOUNG JOHNNY)
Sammy penknife (MR. WILBERFORCE)
Letter from Johnny #1 with envelope (YOUNG SUZY)
Large brown cap (JOHNNY)
2 paintbrushes (ARTIST)
Letter from Johnny #2 in envelope (SUZY)
Letter to Johnny (SUZY)
Small knife (FOOLKILLER)
Whetstone (FOOLKILLER)
Cigarette (CAPTAIN)
Clipboard with recruiting form (CAPTAIN)
Fountain pen (CAPTAIN)
Letter from Johnny #3 (SUZY)
Military duffel bag (JOHNNY)
Large mailbag with mail (WILBUR)
Captain's letter (CAPTAIN, JOHNNY)
Pistol (CAPTAIN)
Rifle (JOHNNY)
Mesh bag of helmets (FOOLKILLER)

Mail carrier's pouch (WILBUR)
4 large manila envelopes (WILBUR)
Boxes of various sizes (WILBUR)
Bundles of letters (WILBUR)
Catalogue (WILBUR)
Constable Byrnes crash box (WILBUR)
Girlie magazines in brown paper (WILBUR)
Letter from Suzy (WILBUR)
Pink envelope with money (WILBUR)
Rubber stamp (WILBUR)
War department telegram (WILBUR)
Box of medals (SENATOR)
Purple heart (SENATOR)
Hospital pillow (JOHNNY)
White sheet (JOHNNY)
Wedding bouquet (WILBUR, SUZY)
2 wedding rings (OLD MINISTER, JOHNNY, SUZY)
Purse (MRS. MILLER)
Rice (BOB)

ACT TWO

Book, Voltaire's *Candide*
Comb (BARBER)
Large white towel (BARBER)
Scissors (BARBER)
Milk bill (JOHNNY)
Bundle of mail (JOHNNY)
Ladies Home Journal magazine (JOHNNY)
Small mailbag (JOHNNY)
Man's wallet (SUZY)
Motorcycle goggles (SUZY, JOHNNY)
Sunglasses (SUZY)
Bassinet with baby (JOHNNY)
Leg irons with ball (WILBUR)
Metal file (WILBUR)
Large Christmas present (BILL)
Basket with knitting (MRS. MILLER)
Blue baby bundle (JOHNNY)
Shopping bag of Christmas presents (SUZY)
Trick or treat bag (JOHN JR.)
2 pair children's sunglasses (JOHN JR, SUZY JR.)
Pink baby bundle (SUZY)
4 paper poppies (MRS. MILLER, BARBER, BILL, BOB)
Children's sheet and blanket (SUZY JR., JOHN JR.)
Pillow (JOHN JR.)
Bag of groceries (SUZY)

Bible (BOB)
Picnic basket with cloth (JOHNNY)
Cane (MRS. MILLER, BOB, JOHNNY, WILBUR)
Blanket (JOHNNY)
Reading glasses (JOHNNY, SUZY)
Needlepoint (JOHNNY)
Late 1970s' newspaper (JOHNNY)
Pillow (SUZY)
2 Easter baskets (JOHNNY)
Flowers for grave (JOHNNY)
Small suitcase (WILBUR)
Waitress pad and pencil (WAITRESS)
Comb (BILL, JOHNNY)
Scissors in case (BILL, BOB)
Birthday cake with many candles (MARGARET)

SOUND EFFECTS

Rooster
Rural morning sounds, then fade
Bicycle bell
Thunder
Rain
Train whistle (circa 1945)
Train pulling out of station (circa 1945)
World War II battle
Rifle shot (circa 1945)
Wedding bells
Gusts of wind
Dog barking
Door bell
Crickets
Plate crashing
Bloodhounds in the distance
Motorcycle starting, idling, fade out
Twittering birds
Wind
Jet plane (1980)